MW00719039

**New Directions for
Teaching and Learning**

Marilla D. Svinicki
EDITOR-IN-CHIEF

R. Eugene Rice
CONSULTING EDITOR

Neither White
Nor Male:
Female Faculty
of Color

Katherine Grace Hendrix
EDITOR

Number 110 • Summer 2007
Jossey-Bass
San Francisco

NEITHER WHITE NOR MALE: FEMALE FACULTY OF COLOR
Katherine Grace Hendrix (ed.)
New Directions for Teaching and Learning, no. 110
Marilla D. Svinicki, Editor-in-Chief
R. Eugene Rice, Consulting Editor

Microfilm copies of issues and articles are available in 16mm and 35mm, as well as microfiche in 105mm, through University Microfilms, Inc., 300 North Zeeb Road, Ann Arbor, Michigan 48106-1346.

NEW DIRECTIONS FOR TEACHING AND LEARNING (ISSN 0271-0633, electronic ISSN 1536-0768) is part of The Jossey-Bass Higher and Adult Education Series and is published quarterly by Wiley Subscription Services, Inc., A Wiley Company, at Jossey-Bass, 989 Market Street, San Francisco, California 94103-1741. Periodicals postage paid at San Francisco, California, and at additional mailing offices. POSTMASTER: Send address changes to New Directions for Teaching and Learning, Jossey-Bass, 989 Market Street, San Francisco, California 94103-1741.

New Directions for Teaching and Learning is indexed in CIJE: Current Index to Journals in Education (ERIC), Contents Pages in Education (T&F), Current Abstracts (EBSCO), Educational Research Abstracts Online (T&F), ERIC Database (Education Resources Information Center), Higher Education Abstracts (Claremont Graduate University), and SCOPUS (Elsevier).

SUBSCRIPTIONS cost $80 for individuals and $195 for institutions, agencies, and libraries in the United States. Prices subject to change. See order form at end of book.

EDITORIAL CORRESPONDENCE should be sent to the editor-in-chief, Marilla D. Svinicki, Department of Educational Psychology, University of Texas at Austin, One University Station, D5800, Austin, TX 78712.

Wiley Bicentennial Logo: Richard J. Pacifico

www.josseybass.com

Contents

EDITOR'S NOTES
Katherine Grace Hendrix

1

1. Cross-Cultural Teaching Apprehension: A Coidentity Approach Toward Minority Teachers
Fang-Yi Flora Wei

5

To understand the advantages and disadvantages of being a young Asian female teacher, the author uses a coidentity analysis to examine teaching styles, the use of language, and self-efficacy beliefs. Given these specific considerations, five pedagogical suggestions for assisting new minority teachers are discussed.

2. Establishing Credibility in the Multicultural Classroom: When the Instructor Speaks with an Accent
Chikako Akamatsu McLean

15

This exploratory research examines how Asian-born female instructors establish teacher credibility in classrooms consisting predominantly of English-speaking American students. Hofstede's cultural dimensions, teacher credibility, and nonverbal immediacy theories are explored. Participant interviews reveal the frequent use of three strategies: self-disclosure, rapport setting, and the elimination of uncertainty.

3. From Behind the Veil: Students' Resistance from Different Directions
Ahlam Muhtaseb

25

Critical race and expectancy violation theories are used to deconstruct students' resistance to a female faculty of color who is a Muslim Arab American wearing the traditional Islamic cover. The author provides a narrative of her teaching experience and describes some techniques used to face such resistance.

4. The Permeable and Impermeable Wall of Expectations
Mary Fong

35

Twenty-five years of a Chinese American woman's experience in higher education at universities in Southern California and the Pacific Northwest are presented by discussing her career in four stages: master's level teaching assistant, part-time instructor, doctoral teaching assistant, and professor.

5. You Can't "De-Race" and "De-Womanize" Me: Experiences   45
When You Go Global
Aparna G. Hebbani
Race matters in the classroom when you are a minority female faculty
member. This chapter addresses the issue from the author's perspective
of having taught for several years in the United States and then expand-
ing her horizons by teaching in Australia, Malaysia, and Hong Kong as
well as globally via distance education. The concluding section discusses the emergence of the adaptive female academic of color who successfully balances a happy work and family life.

6. Black Feminist Thought and Cultural Contracts: 55
Understanding the Intersection and Negotiation of Racial,
Gendered, and Professional Identities in the Academy
Tina M. Harris
This chapter explores identity negotiation by women of color in academe at a predominantly white institution. The author discusses use of
the title *doctor* as a form of address to manage interactions with graduate students in the college classroom. The difficulties associated with
negotiating and balancing diverse and complex identities in an oppressive context are also addressed.

7. Being an Interculturally Competent Instructor in the United   65
States: Issues of Classroom Dynamics and Appropriateness, and
Recommendations for International Instructors
Claudia Ladeira McCalman
This chapter addresses the increasing internationalization of classrooms
in the United States, points out resistance to and challenges of this
internationalization process, and suggests strategies to narrow the cultural gap between instructors and undergraduates. The author calls
other international and women of color to establish a base of support
to overcome their challenges in academia.

8. Women of Color Teaching Students of Color: Creating an   75
Effective Classroom Climate Through Caring, Challenging,
and Consulting
Dora E. Saavedra and Marisa L. Saavedra
Two faculty women of color discuss three pedagogical tools (caring,
challenging, and consulting) that they use to create a classroom climate
designed to enhance Hispanic students' success by engaging and motivating them to succeed in one of the poorest areas of the country.

9. "She Must Be Trippin'": The Secret of Disrespect from   85
Students of Color Toward Faculty of Color
Katherine Grace Hendrix
The author introduces literature regarding female faculty, student
aggression, classroom incivility, and racial identity development in
order to analyze the potential sources of disrespectful behavior coming
not from white students but from some students of one's own race or
ethnicity. One goal is to break the silence regarding this particular type
of resistance to professorial authority.

10. Epilogue   97
Katherine Grace Hendrix
A brief synthesis connects the teaching experiences of ten female faculty of color—the authors of this volume's nine chapters—that transcend race and nationality.

INDEX   99

FROM THE SERIES EDITOR

About This Publication. Since 1980, *New Directions for Teaching and Learning (NDTL)* has brought a unique blend of theory, research, and practice to leaders in postsecondary education. *NDTL* sourcebooks strive not only for solid substance but also for timeliness, compactness, and accessibility.

The series has four goals: to inform readers about current and future directions in teaching and learning in postsecondary education, to illuminate the context that shapes these new directions, to illustrate these new directions through examples from real settings, and to propose ways in which these new directions can be incorporated into still other settings.

This publication reflects the view that teaching deserves respect as a high form of scholarship. We believe that significant scholarship is conducted not only by researchers who report results of empirical investigations but also by practitioners who share the discipline's reflections about teaching. Contributors to *NDTL* approach questions of teaching and learning as seriously as they approach substantive questions in their own disciplines, and they deal not only with pedagogical issues but also with the intellectual and social context in which these issues arise. Authors deal on the one hand with theory and research and on the other with practice, and they translate from research and theory to practice and back again.

About This Volume. The ability to see our context through the eyes of another is an important first step toward understanding. This issue gives a much-needed window into the experiences of faculty women of color in order to better understand the environment in which they work from both a personal and a theoretical perspective. Perhaps this window will open the way for more support and understanding in both directions.

Marilla D. Svinicki
Editor-in-Chief

MARILLA D. SVINICKI is associate professor of educational psychology at the University of Texas at Austin.

Editor's Notes

This issue of *New Directions for Teaching and Learning* brings together ten women of color who represent a wide range of years of teaching experience, regions of teaching, types of higher education institution, administrative experiences, communication subspecialties, nationalities, races and ethnicities, and ages. According to Harvey (2002), in 1999 85.6 percent of U.S. full-time faculty were white whereas 14.4 percent were minority, and there was a 28.3 percent increase in the number of minority faculty from 1991 to 1999, with women of color nearly doubling in number during those eight years.

Over the past two decades, scholars (primarily those of color) have gradually begun to investigate the experience of being faculty of color, especially in predominantly white institutions of higher education (Brown, 1994; Foster, 1990; Gonzalez, Houston, and Chen, 2000; Hendrix, Jackson, and Warren, 2003; Hidalgo, McDowell, and Siddle, 1990; Knowles and Harleston, 1997). A growing body of literature reflects the lived experience of faculty of color in some disciplines (such as education) while researchers in other fields continue to operate within a paradigm in which the study of faculty, graduate, and undergraduate students of color falls outside of designated areas of "legitimate" investigation. In such disciplines, the researcher's axiological position values the study of one group to the exclusion of others—namely, faculty of color. In addition, there is an implicit (and until recently largely uncontested) assumption that the experiences of white faculty generalize to faculty of color.

An additional concern is that the research that does exist on faculty of color, although important, tends to focus only on one particular race, ethnicity, or nationality. As a result, prior research gives a glimpse into the experience of one demographic group of faculty in the postsecondary classroom but leaves the reader to wonder whether minority faculty from other cultural groups may share similar or divergent experiences. Given the limited information on the academic experience in general and the particular pedagogical strategies and strengths of faculty of color, the scholars in this issue of *New Directions for Learning and Teaching* come together to begin the process of articulating the academic experiences of female professors of color. While chronicling our challenges within academia as well as our contributions to the education of U.S. students, this collaborative effort also adds depth to the existing literature on faculty of color, serves as a reference for positioning women of color within the larger context of higher education (moving us from margin to center), and lays a foundation for more inclusive future research.

New Directions for Teaching and Learning, no. 110, Summer 2007   © Wiley Periodicals, Inc.
Published online in Wiley InterScience (www.interscience.wiley.com) • DOI: 10.1002/tl.268

1

The first five chapters provide the reader with a view of the classroom based on the experiences of one self-described Arab and four ethnically diverse Asian female faculty teaching in U.S. classrooms (and in the case of Hebbani, international classrooms), all of whom are marked by the accented speech of their respective native languages (that is, Chinese, Cantonese, Japanese, Arabic, Mandarin, and Kannada). In Chapters One, Two, and Three the scholars incorporate several theories (Hofstede's cultural dimensions, expectancy violation theory, critical race theory, and worldview) to bolster their autoethnographic depictions of their classroom challenges and contributions. Chapter Four moves the reader from the vantage point of international faculty to that of a U.S.-born female faculty member of color; and finally, in Chapter Five, Hebbani expands the classroom context beyond U.S. borders to incorporate her experience of moving from a position of "other" teaching in the United States to teaching in Australia, Hong Kong, and Malaysia. Harris, in Chapter Six, then explores the construct of double consciousness as applied to race and gender when teaching as a black woman in a predominately white institution. McCalman supplements the macrodiscussion of a colored presence in the classroom by using Intercultural Communication Competence as a concept capable of allowing international faculty of color (in her case, a Brazilian) to bridge the gap between student and teacher—in essence communicating in a manner that appears less "foreign" to one's students. In Chapter Eight the Saavedras more directly articulate the Hispanic experience by discussing how to foster mentoring relationships when teaching Hispanic students within South Texas higher educational systems. Finally, in Chapter Nine Hendrix addresses the less palpable and more concealed topic of classroom opposition from students of color.

The issue's nine chapters are followed by a brief synthesis connecting the teaching experiences of these ten female faculty of color—experiences that transcend race and nationality and thereby bind these women together into a special relationship of sisterhood marked by interracial and interethnic friendship, mentorship, and womanhood.

Katherine Grace Hendrix
Editor

References

Brown, S. V. "The Impasse on Faculty Diversity in Higher Education: A National Agenda." In M. J. Justiz, R. Wilson, and L. G. Bjork (eds.), *Minorities in Higher Education*. Phoenix, Ariz.: Oryx Press, 1994.

Foster, M. "The Politics of Race: Through the Eyes of African-American Teachers." *Journal of Education*, 1990, *172*, 123–141.

Gonzalez, A., Houston, M., and Chen, C. (eds.). *Our Voices: Essays in Culture, Ethnicity, and Communication*. (3rd ed.) Los Angeles: Roxbury, 2000.

Harvey, W. B. *Minorities in Higher Education 2001–2002: Nineteenth Annual Status Report*. Washington, D.C.: American Council on Education, Office of Minorities in Higher Education, 2002.

Hendrix, K. G., Jackson, R., II, and Warren, J. "Shifting Academic Landscapes: Exploring Co-Identities, Identity Negotiation and Critical Progressive Pedagogy. *Communication Education,* 2003, *52,* 177–190.

Hidalgo, N. M., McDowell, C. L., and Siddle, E. V. (eds.). *Facing Racism in Education.* Cambridge, Mass.: Harvard Educational Review, 1990.

Knowles, M. F., and Harleston, B. W. *Achieving Diversity in the Professoriate: Challenges and Opportunities.* Washington, D.C.: American Council on Education, 1997.

KATHERINE GRACE HENDRIX *is associate professor and former basic course director in the Department of Communication at the University of Memphis. She examines classroom credibility and the epistemological and axiological positions of research communities from a critical perspective.*

NEW DIRECTIONS FOR TEACHING AND LEARNING • DOI: 10.1002/tl

1

Teaching apprehension is used to frame the author's anxiety about being a young Asian female teacher in a four-year research-oriented university. The chapter explores how demographic characteristics influence teaching styles, the use of language, and self-efficacy beliefs.

Cross-Cultural Teaching Apprehension: A Coidentity Approach Toward Minority Teachers

Fang-Yi Flora Wei

From reading my students' e-mails and essays I have learned to understand better my identity as a young Asian female instructor at the university level. I insist on my students' usage of *he or she* rather than *he* alone in their writing because males and females should receive equal recognition in today's society. However, some students may falsely assume that I am attempting to degrade males' identity. When my students write to me, many of them habitually begin with "Hi, Mrs. Wei." Because I want to respond politely to my students' messages I am unwilling to correct them and explain that Wei is *my* family name rather than my husband's. Yet my students have no difficulty applying appropriate titles to male teachers. To show their respect to male professors, most college students are comfortable using *Dr.* before the male teachers' family names. More specifically, if I present my interest in conducting research, students are surprised that a female college teacher's duty is not limited to teaching classes. A female instructor is not seen as having the role of researcher and teacher simultaneously; as a result, students have difficulty accepting that image of female faculty.

In terms of students' perceptions of a nonnative speaker's teaching, students with little experience with foreign instructors have a difficult time

I thank my dedicated mentor, Katherine Grace Hendrix, for providing insightful comments and suggestions about this manuscript.

accepting foreign teachers' guidance. As an Asian and nonnative speaker, I have found a few students to have difficulty accepting my sincere critiques, such as when I taught a public speaking course. Some students have either used my foreign-accented speech as an excuse for lowering their learning standards or assumed that I had insufficient knowledge to teach the course due to my ethnicity.[1] In comparison, little conflict takes place when I teach quantitative research methods because this course requires students to use statistical analyses. This phenomenon derives from U.S. students' stereotype that all Asian teachers are mathematical geniuses who can play with arithmetic easily. Consequently, U.S. students tend to give more recognition to Asian professors' mathematical developments and as a result are more willing to accept my professional identity when I teach science-oriented subjects than when I teach language-oriented subjects. Although I enjoy teaching quantitative research methods, I pondered the question, Do students respect me in the quantitative class because of my professional identity or because of their stereotype of Asians?

My identity as a teacher is more complicated than that of most females and Asians because I am younger than thirty years old. On first meeting students every semester, I sense their inordinate or indifferent eye contact. These two types of eye contact did not mean anything to me until I accidentally heard some students talking in whispers, saying, "She's young and skinny." My intuition told me that students might judge my teaching ability on the basis of my physical appearance. To provide open communication in my classroom, I intentionally made eye contact with all of the students and kindly asked whether they were nervous about taking this class. As I was waiting for them to articulate their concerns, a male student suddenly raised his hand and stated, "You know, you look very young." The entire class became silent, waiting to hear my response to his statement.

As a woman, in most social occasions I appreciate someone still considering me "young" rather than "old." But as a college instructor in a classroom setting, I interpret this appraisal differently. The adjective *young* in this case contains a negative connotation of being inexperienced, and students may use it to challenge a teacher's knowledge, authority, and limitations. At that moment I hoped to challenge this male student intellectually but not create any negative feelings. To shift my students' negative attention away from my academic identity and to decrease their anxiety, I said laughingly, "Thank you for your compliment, which shows that I did not waste my makeup." Even though this response made my students smile, their reactions inspired me to consider the potential advantages and disadvantages of being a young minority female instructor.

My personal experiences may not suggest that all females are underrepresented in the academic profession, but my ethnicity encourages me to reconsider the teaching experience of female faculty members. I therefore begin by reviewing the academic experiences of female minority faculty members in three areas: (1) gender and teaching, (2) ethnicity and teaching, and (3) age and teaching. The purpose of this chapter is to discuss how demographic characteristics relate to teaching styles and language, and how these in turn may reshape our self-efficacy beliefs and decrease our teaching apprehension in academia.

Academic Experiences of Female Minority Faculty

A great number of female instructors receive few positive and satisfied student responses to their teaching (Hamilton, 2002). Many scholars (such as Basow, Phelan, and Capotosto, 2006; Bennett, 1982; Harris, 1975; Sandler, 1991) have discussed their research regarding whether a gender-biased climate exists for female instructors' teaching, as well as whether below-average student evaluations result from cultural differences between masculine and feminine teaching styles. Studies have shown that male students tend to give female instructors lower ratings in teaching and credibility than they give male instructors (Basow, 1995; Basow and Silberg, 1987; Hargett, 1999). Fewer academic positions and promotions are provided to female faculty in most research and doctoral-granting universities (Ethington, Smart, and Zeltman, 1989; Kuck, Marzabadi, and Nolan, 2004). Furthermore, Liu and Meyer (2005) found that minority teachers, on average, have to deal with more student discipline problems than do Caucasian teachers. Hendrix (1997) pointed out that U.S. students challenge African American teachers' credibility more commonly than they challenge the credibility of Caucasian teachers. Thus the hidden issue centers around not only whether we as female college teachers experience a chilly climate but also how we as female minority instructors have to establish our credibility in order to interact with students while teaching. De Simone (2001) pointed out that teaching is a process of forming our individual identities, and that we learn who we are through social interactions; consequently, college teachers may evolve differently from one another on the basis of their self-awareness. As teachers, we do not have the power to manipulate which identities are desirable, and students cannot define every meaning for us in classroom communication. To build a supportive learning environment, teachers and students have to work together to establish the preferable norm. We learn to negotiate an acceptable pedagogy as well as our professional identities in different academic settings (Hendrix, Jackson, and Warren, 2003). Given this specific consideration, I now discuss whether there are gender-related differences among teachers.

Gender and Teaching. In regard to whether there are gender-related differences among teachers, the central issue is not whether one gender is more talented than the other relative to a particular teaching position; instead, it is a matter of whether male and female faculty might be more comfortable using one particular teaching style rather than another. Centra and Gaubatz (2000) found that male instructors preferred to use lecture methods whereas females preferred to use discussions. Regarding course organization, male students rated male instructors as more organized than female teachers whereas female students believed that female instructors were more interactive in their teaching. When Goodwin and Stevens (1993) investigated what ideas construct faculty members' perceptions of "good" teaching, the results showed that most female professors were more concerned than male professors about students' cognitive thinking and self-esteem. These studies show then that women are not less talented than men in teaching. If there are differences between how males and females teach, they might be those differences identified in the students' observations: that females are more interactive and expressive in communication than males, and that males are more direct and organized in presenting messages than females. Thus male instructors may be more likely than female instructors to receive compliments for being effective teachers in the undergraduate and lecture-oriented teaching format. Female instructors, then, in order to be effective, should make adaptations for students not only in teaching styles but also in the use of language.

How we use language shapes our identities in classroom communication, and males and females use language differently to represent their cultures. Kirtley and Weaver (1999) found that women prefer to use a socially oriented style of communication whereas men prefer to use a results-oriented style of communication. As Basow and Rubenfeld (2003, p. 183) have pointed out, "Women are thought to use more expressive, tentative, and polite language than men do." Based on different identities, men's talk might demonstrate more authority or be more direct than women's talk. Although no evidence indicates that the frequent use of expressive, tentative, and polite language influences the leadership abilities of female faculty, I believe that these traits may contribute to male and female instructors' credibility being evaluated differently. Female instructors might promote a supportive image by using polite language. The use of expressive and polite language helps the instructor build a friendly relationship with students. However, students might misinterpret a female instructor's politeness as softness. To avoid hurting or offending students, female instructors are more likely to say, "You can improve this. Why don't you work some more on it?" We may avoid saying, "Your paper is not acceptable and you have to rewrite it." The term *not acceptable* demonstrates our authority; however, we are unwilling to display it in most situations (see Tannen, 1994). These observations suggest that female teachers' comfortableness with using polite language leads us to be easily challenged and misunderstood by students and colleagues. Our problems are not all derived from the use of polite language, however. Ethnicity is another considerable factor.

Ethnicity and Teaching. With respect to ethnicity, Fitch and Morgan (2003) found that college students had negative perceptions of native speakers' ability to express themselves. These observations not only indicate that minority teachers are less appreciated by college students than are "native" instructors, but also suggest that there are cultural language barriers between students and teachers in classroom communication.

Language is power, but for international teachers, language is a barrier. My personal teaching experience suggests that there is a difference between formal and informal talk. When native speakers describe their thoughts, they are very comfortable using slang or reductions to explain what they mean. However, most second-language speakers learned to speak English in the most formal and polite ways; therefore we may have difficulty imitating or understanding a native speaker's informal speaking style. For example, one of my students said, "You rock!" to other students in a classroom discussion. At that moment my mind went blank for about three seconds as I attempted to recall the meaning of that phrase. I had no firm understanding of it because my colleagues never used it in their conversations. Second-language speakers tend to interact formally rather than informally in the workplace; in contrast, college students enjoy using informal talk to ask questions and express their ideas.

Age and Teaching. Regardless of gender or cultural differences, aging is an inevitable process for everyone. Smith (2001), a male professor, pointed out his feelings by saying, "While everyone else in the room is the same youthful age my students have always been, I am all-too-visibly getting older" (p. B1). Although I have not yet experienced the disadvantages of being an "old" college teacher, one advantage of being a young teacher is that I am more sensitive to my students' perspectives and feelings.[2] I gained my first teaching experience as a graduate teaching assistant (GTA). Graduate students working as GTAs may psychologically visualize an integrative coidentity of both teacher and student. This former double identity of teacher and graduate student influences my current sensitivity and patience toward students' needs even though they may make less adequate comments and raise less intelligent questions than graduate students in class. I can connect to their attitudes and behaviors as if I were a college student. I do not perceive that I have to be a superior; instead, I act as a friend in classroom discussion.[3] Sensenbaugh (1995) noted that building interpersonal relationships involving friendliness, creativity, and accessibility is an important factor in GTAs' teaching. Sensenbaugh's study also suggests that when college students connect to their teachers' perspectives, they may consider their relationship with the teacher to be more supportive of the learning experience.

Although college students may consider a friendly relationship with the instructor, the reason one instructor is rated high is different from the reason another instructor is rated low. For instance, Edwards and Harwood (2003) found that undergraduate students are likely to rate older instructors rather than younger instructors as effective teachers because older instructors are traditionally perceived as wise and competent in the subject and younger instructors are perceived as less experienced and confident in teaching. Considering this difference, the other disadvantage of being a young instructor is emotional exhaustion. Lackritz (2004) suggests that there is a negative correlation between faculty members' emotional exhaustion and their age. Younger faculty members tend to have more career pressures than do older faculty members. This result reflects my first year of teaching, which was filled not only with new coursework preparation but also with learning to adjust to the role of being an imperfect teacher. The psychological pressure derived from the question, "Am I good enough in my teaching?" Because of the aspiration to be a good teacher, whatever happened during a class period easily became the focus of my day. During the lunch break I kept thinking about my teaching and my students' attitudes; I kept asking myself why two students were absent that day and whether they enjoyed my teaching.

In addition to the psychological pressure, students' comments on evaluations may unintentionally manipulate a young teacher's classroom policy, interaction, and confidence. In comparison to older faculty, a new teacher is very vulnerable to negative criticism. Young teachers depend on students' feedback on the evaluations rather than on their own cumulative teaching experiences and confidence to determine their identities.

Discussion

Female instructors are not less professional and talented than male instructors; instead, we use different teaching and language styles to negotiate our identities in academia. Because teaching experiences and peer and student evaluations have a sequential influence on an instructor's self-efficacy, the most important lesson is learning how to refine the self-efficacy of female faculty members. *Teacher self-efficacy* is defined as an instructor's belief in his or her ability to perform academia-related tasks (Mottet, Beebe, Raffeld, and Medlock, 2004). Schoen and Winocur (1988) found that females have more confidence in teaching than in conducting research. Although women are as professional as men in the academic profession, previous studies (such as Sampson, 1987; Schneider, 1998) have indicated that women do not apply for promotion because they believe they do not have sufficient experience or enough publications. Vasil (1996) found that male professors tend to have stronger self-efficacy beliefs than females with respect to self-promoting strategies. Park (1996) suggested that females might focus more on teaching and service than on research; however, when tenure and promotion are judged by a committee, the committee may not weigh teaching over research.

Furthermore, as Goodwin and Stevens (1993) have pointed out, "female professors seem to place greater value than male professors on seeking 'outside' help from peers and others" (p. 181). Whether female professors can gain support from peers as much as male professors can is questionable. The dilemma for females in contrast to males is that in academia a limited number of senior female mentors are available, and most male mentors avoid mentoring females because they fear getting involved in sexual rumors or they perceive women's attitudes toward the academic profession as less serious than those of men (Luna and Cullen, 1995). Because they receive limited assistance in a highly competitive environment, it is difficult for female faculty members to cultivate a strong self-efficacy, and without receiving senior faculty members' sincere guidance, it is difficult for female faculty members to believe they can survive in academia.

Practical Implications

The goal of this chapter has been to disclose the unheard voice of young minority female instructors. Regardless of our individual identities, facilitating our students' learning is a primary goal of our teaching. As a young Asian female instructor, I suggest the following five pedagogical adjustments for overcoming our fear and apprehension about teaching:

1. We must emphasize an academic age defined by our professional knowledge rather than by our biological age.
2. Asking mentors' opinions is an important method for relieving internal anxiety and building academic rapport.
3. When using student evaluations to measure our teaching effectiveness, we should be sensitive to what students say; however, we should not act on any oversensitive reactions we have to these comments (see Hendrix, 2000).
4. We should not limit our communication styles to those based on a single cultural identity.
5. Although better research may not always produce better teaching (Park, 1996), females should recognize their potential to be good researchers.

First, we may encounter in our students' eyes different evaluations of being young. Although students may have less confidence in younger instructors' teaching than in the teaching of older instructors, we can work positively to accelerate our academic age by receiving external training, gaining a mentor's guidance, and reading about teaching in other sources. Second, emotional burnout rates for young, female instructors tend to be high (Lackritz, 2004). To gain emotional support, we need to have reliable mentors who can understand our difficulties and provide helpful suggestions. Third, because many external factors (such as class size and the personalities of male and female students) can influence rating results, students in a large class tend to give the instructor a poorer evaluation than do students in a small class (Centra and Gaubatz, 2000). A single negative comment is insufficient to represent *every* student's opinion, and a couple of students with hostility may skew the ratings on the evaluations. We must not trust every comment on the evaluations. Next, the vital issue is not whether we are males or females, native or nonnative speakers; instead, it is whether we are comfortable and confident in our communication styles in a multicultural classroom. In turn, by using language appropriately, we can produce desirable teaching outcomes and limit our apprehension about teaching. Finally, we aspire to be good researchers, not because we are subordinates in a male-oriented culture or research-oriented institution, but because we are motivated to enrich students' learning by sharing what we know and have found in our research.

Conclusion

As a young minority female college teacher, I am anxious about predicting my career path as well as about finding my identity in my students' eyes. Through their eyes I have observed my teaching transition from an inept debut to a more skilled delivery. I do not think that a female scholar needs to sacrifice all feminine characteristics and wear a masculine mask in an academic environment; however, an inexperienced minority female faculty member has to learn to negotiate persistently with students and colleagues about her professional identity, strengths, difficulties, and expectations for the future. The challenge for us is not whether we should devote our time and energy to teaching classes, conducting research, or taking care of family; instead, it is whether we have the courage and fair access to pursue a desirable career in academia.

Notes

1. Students might like to use their instructors as role models in learning.
2. One advantage that older Caucasian teachers have is that they have more power and teaching credibility in academia, and students are less likely to challenge their authority and limitations.
3. The great risk for young instructors of establishing a friendly image in their teaching is losing authority. To balance this approach, young instructors need also to be firm in classroom policies.

References

Basow, S. A. "Student Evaluations of College Professors When Gender Matters." *Journal of Educational Psychology*, 1995, 87, 656–665.
Basow, S. A., Phelan, J. E., and Capotosto, L. "Gender Patterns in College Students' Choices of their Best and Worst Professors." *Psychology of Women Quarterly*, 2006, 30, 25–35.
Basow, S. A., and Rubenfeld, K. "'Troubles Talk': Effects of Gender and Gender Typing." *Sex Roles: A Journal of Research*, 2003, 51, 183–187.
Basow, S. A., and Silberg, N. T. "Student Evaluations of College Professors: Are Female and Male Professors Rated Differently?" *Journal of Educational Psychology*, 1987, 70, 308–314.
Bennett, S. K. "Student Perceptions of and Expectations for Male and Female Instructors: Evidence Relating to the Question of Gender Bias in Teaching Evaluation." *Journal of Educational Psychology*, 1982, 74, 170–179.

Centra, J. A., and Gaubatz, N. B. "Is There Gender Bias in Student Evaluations of Teaching?" *Journal of Higher Education*, 2000, *70*, 17–33.

De Simone, D. M. "Identity of the University Professor Is Formulated over Time, Requiring Self-Discovery Followed by Being an Intellectual Scholar and Teacher." *Education*, 2001, *122*, 283–295.

Edwards, C., and Harwood, J. "Social Identity in the Classroom: An Examination of Age Identification Between Students and Instructors." *Communication Education*, 2003, *52*, 60–65.

Ethington, C. A., Smart, J. C., and Zeltmann, M. L. "Institutional and Departmental Satisfaction of Women Faculty." *Research in Higher Education*, 1989, *30*, 261–271.

Fitch, F., and Morgan, S. E. "Not a Lick of English": Constructing the ITA Identity Through Student Narratives." *Communication Education*, 2003, *52*, 297–310.

Goodwin, L. D., and Stevens, E. A. "The Influence of Gender on University Faculty Members' Perceptions of "Good" Teaching." *Journal of Higher Education*, 1993, *64*, 166–185.

Hamilton, K. "Race in the College Classroom: Minority Faculty Often Face Student Resistance When Teaching About Race." *Black Issues in Higher Education*, 2002, *19*, 32–36.

Hargett, J. "Student Perceptions of Male and Female Instructor Level of Immediacy and Teacher Credibility." *Women and Language*, 1999, *22*, 46.

Harris, M. B. "Sex Role Stereotypes and Teacher Evaluations." *Journal of Educational Psychology*, 1975, *67*, 751–756.

Hendrix, K. G. "Student Perceptions of Verbal and Nonverbal Cues Leading to Images of Black and White Professor Credibility." *The Howard Journal of Communications*, 1997, *8*, 251–273.

Hendrix, K. G. *The Teaching Assistant's Guide to the Basic Course.* Belmont, Calif.: Wadsworth, 2000.

Hendrix, K. G., Jackson, R. L., II, and Warren, J. R. "Shifting Academic Landscapes: Exploring Co-Identities, Identity Negotiation, and Critical Progressive Pedagogy." *Communication Education*, 2003, *52*, 177–190.

Kirtley, M. D., and Weaver, J. B. "Exploring the Impact of Gender Role Self-Perception on Communication Style." *Women's Studies in Communication*, 1999, *22*, 190–209.

Kuck, V. J., Marzabadi, C. H., and Nolan, S. A. "Analysis by Gender of Doctoral and Postdoctoral Institution of Faculty Members at the Top Fifty Ranked Chemistry Departments." *Journal of Chemical Education*, 2004, *81*, 356–363.

Lackritz, J. R. "Exploring Burnout Among University Faculty: Incidence, Performance, and Demographic Issues." *Teaching and Teacher Education*, 2004, *20*, 713–729.

Liu, S. X., and Meyer, J. P. "Teachers' Perceptions of Their Jobs: A Multilevel Analysis of Teacher Follow-Up Survey for 1994–95." *Teachers College Record*, 2005, *107*, 985–1003.

Luna, G., and Cullen, D. L. "Empowering the Faculty: Mentoring Redirected and Renewed." *ASHE-ERIC Higher Education Reports*, 1995, *3*, 1–87.

Mottet, T. P., Beebe, S. A., Raffeld, P. C., and Medlock, A. L. "The Effects of Student Verbal and Nonverbal Responsiveness on Teacher Self-Efficacy and Job Satisfaction." *Communication Education*, 2004, *53*, 150–163.

Park, S. M. "Research, Teaching, and Service: Why Shouldn't Women's Work Count?" *Journal of Higher Education*, 1996, *67*, 46–84.

Sampson, S. N. "Equal Opportunity, Alone, Is Not Enough or Why There Are More Male Principals in Schools These Days." *Australian Journal of Education*, 1987, *31*, 27–42.

Sandler, B. "Women Faculty at Work in the Classroom, or Why It Still Hurts to Be a Woman in Labor." *Communication Education*, 1991, *40*, 6–15.

Schneider, A. "Why Don't Women Publish as Much as Men?" *Chronicle of Higher Education*, 1998, *45*, A14–16.

Schoen, L. G., and Winocur, S. "An Investigation of the Self-Efficacy of Male and Female Academics." *Journal of Vocational Behavior*, 1988, *32*, 307–320.

Sensenbaugh, R. "How Effective Communication Can Enhance Teaching at the College

Level." Bloomington, Ind.: ERIC Clearinghouse on Reading English and Communication, 1995. (ED380847) Retrieved October 25, 2005, from http://www.eric.edu.gov

Smith, C. "When a Professor Ages . . . and His Students Don't." *Chronicle of Higher Education,* Feb. 9, 2001, Article B20. Retrieved October 25, 2005, from http://chronicle.com/weekly/v47/i22/22b02001.htm

Tannen, D. *Talking from 9 to 5: How Women's and Men's Conversational Styles Affect Who Gets Heard, Who Gets Credit, and What Gets Done at Work.* New York: Morrow, 1994.

Vasil, L. "Social Process Skills and Career Achievement Among Male and Female Academics." *Journal of Higher Education,* 1996, 67, 103–114.

FANG-YI FLORA WEI is visiting assistant professor of communication at the University of Kentucky.

Applying theories of cultural dimensions, teacher credibility, and nonverbal immediacy, this chapter explores classroom management techniques used by Asian female teachers to establish credibility.

Establishing Credibility in the Multicultural Classroom: When the Instructor Speaks with an Accent

Chikako Akamatsu McLean

As cultural diversity in higher education increases nationwide, community colleges are working with a kaleidoscope of student demographics. Teaching communication courses in such settings presents a great challenge; this challenge is compounded when the instructor is an Asian-born female with an accent. When Asian-born instructors teach communication-related courses to a predominantly native English-speaking student body, our credibility is subject to challenge. My frequent conversations with other female Asian instructors have confirmed that we initially sense skepticism among the students due to our nonnative background. However, we believe that because of our background we can provide a unique "outside-in" viewpoint on the American culture.

Geert Hofstede's work (1980) in intercultural communication forms a guidebook for developing the outside-in viewpoint that Asian female instructors need. The cultural dimensions he suggested clarify the characteristics of U.S. classrooms. His analyses of the world's cultures focus on *how* rather than *what* we think, feel, and act in organizations. Awareness of such analyses may be useful for Asian female academics entering U.S. higher education. Knowing how to establish teacher credibility in the United States is also a key element in increasing effectiveness in predominantly Caucasian classrooms. The classroom management techniques of female Asian teachers will likely

follow their own cultural frame of reference; therefore, understanding non-verbal immediacy theory (Teven and Hanson, 2004; Johnson and Miller, 2002) may be useful as a third resource in assessing our effectiveness in the classroom.

Using Hofstede's cultural dimensions, teacher credibility theory, and nonverbal immediacy theory, I conducted an exploratory study investigating how female Asian-born college faculty establish their credibility with native-speaker students.

Cultural Dimensions and Their Application to the Classroom

From 1967 to 1973, Hofstede (1980) conducted a groundbreaking study of correlations and connections between cultural backgrounds and work-related value patterns among employees of IBM from around the world. He scored the results from fifty-three cultures and placed them on a continuum, identifying four cultural dimensions: *individualism-collectivism, power distance, uncertainty avoidance,* and *masculinity.* These dimensions can be applied not only to the corporation's organizational strategies but also to the field of education. For example, in a teacher training class, Hofstede observed a Dutch teacher applying more structure in his classroom management for a group of Asian students than the teacher was accustomed to using. By adopting methods considered inappropriate in the standards of his native culture, the Dutch teacher successfully bridged the cross-cultural teaching gap (Hofstede, 1986).

Individualism-Collectivism. According to Hofstede (1991), *individualism* pertains to societies with loose ties between individuals while *collectivism* reflects strong, cohesive in-groups. In U.S. classrooms, the individualism-collectivism dimension can be directly related to such student activities as group projects. Due to the strong in-group and out-group distinction, students from collectivist countries hesitate to speak up in larger groups, especially with strangers they perceive as members of the out-group; but the hesitation decreases in smaller groups (Hofstede, 1991).

Uncertainty Avoidance. *Uncertainty avoidance* is defined as the level of tolerance toward uncertainty and ambiguity within a society. Hofstede (1991) observed that students in cultures with strong uncertainty avoidance preferred highly structured classroom practices while students from cultures with weak uncertainty avoidance were more susceptible to flexible and accommodating approaches. According to Hofstede, students from strong uncertainty avoidance countries, such as Japan, expect their teacher to be the expert. Intellectual disagreement from a student is disrespectful and viewed as disloyalty toward the teacher. Conversely, in classrooms with students from weak uncertainty avoidance countries, such as the United States, an intellectual disagreement may be regarded as a stimulating exercise. Teacher credibility tends to increase when teachers encourage honest response and disagreement in class; at the same time, students are likely to feel comfortable arguing points with the teacher without feeling disrespectful.

Power Distance. Hofstede (1991) defined *power distance* as the level of tolerance toward inequalities of power and wealth within a society. In high power-distance cultures, the classroom becomes "teacher-centered with strict orders" (p. 34). However, in low power-distance cultures, the educational process is student centered, encouraging mutual communication between teachers and students. For example, American teachers in a classroom of Japanese students often experience little feedback from the students until they call out a student's name and ask for feedback. Eventually, the teachers may have to give up their customary reliance on student feedback to assess classroom effectiveness, leaving them without an important pedagogical tool.

Masculinity. Hofstede (1991) listed key differences between feminine and masculine societies in their general norms for family, school, and workplace. In masculine societies, such as Japan, the best student is the norm, and failing in school is unacceptable. Excellence in student achievements is rewarded, and teachers' excellence is appreciated. In feminine societies, the average student is the norm, and failing in school is a minor incident. Friendliness of teachers is valued, and social skills and students' social adaptation are emphasized.

Application of Cultural Dimensions

As just described, Hofstede's cultural dimensions form a strong framework for education (1986). The individualism-collectivism spectrum can be applied to leadership styles and effectiveness in small group communication. While uncertainty avoidance explains the communication patterns between teacher and students, power distance illustrates students' expectations of the teacher's classroom management techniques. Finally, the masculinity dimension depicts the contrast between academic achievements and social skills in education.

For Asian-born female teachers of U.S. students, this information regarding cultural dimensions may be particularly useful when designing assignments, class activities, and evaluation, and in setting the classroom atmosphere. While cautiously avoiding stereotyping, these teachers are more likely to connect with U.S. students, and consequently to gain respect, when they are in tune with the cultural backgrounds of the students. Each dimension influences teacher credibility. Without credibility a teacher fails.

Application in Academia: Teacher Credibility

In contemporary research in social science disciplines, McCroskey, Holdridge, and Toomb (1974) defined teacher credibility as a composite of character, sociability, composure, extroversion, and competence. McCroskey (1992) further suggested that the teacher's credibility was determined in three primary dimensions: caring, competence, and trustworthiness. Positive teacher credibility can also be measured by such behavioral parameters as verbal and nonverbal immediacy (Johnson and Miller, 2002), nonverbal immediacy and perceived caring (Teven and Hanson, 2004), and affinity seeking (Frymier and Thompson, 1992).

Nonverbal Immediacy

Teacher *immediacy* refers to teachers' verbal and nonverbal communication attempting to reduce the physical and psychological distance between teachers and students (Andersen, 1979; Gorham, 1988). The importance of understanding the use of nonverbal message systems has long been recognized; their functions are referred to as a *silent language* (Hall, 1959). Hall and Hall (1987) asserted that because nonverbal message systems differ in each culture, cultural communications are deeper and more complex than mere verbal messages. Considering this cross-cultural element in teacher-student communication, Neuliep (1997) suggested that although students from a low-context culture (such as the United States) recognized certain teacher behaviors as immediate, students from a high-context culture (such as Japan) might not. The possible discrepancies in perceptions of nonverbal communicative behaviors between the United States and other cultures may hamper the female Asian instructor new to the United States because she cannot count on her American students interpreting her behavior in the same way as Asian students would.

When Asian-born female teachers are deprived of highly contextual, low-immediate communication practices, they are more likely to face confusion, frustration, and apprehension over their effectiveness in the classroom. Likewise, when American students are denied verbal and high-immediate interactions with teachers during class sessions, their perception of the Asian-born teacher's credibility may drastically deteriorate, causing disharmony between the teacher and the students. By investigating how Asian-born female faculty find ways to overcome such cross-cultural issues, we may find insights into how Asian-born female teachers of communication can make a smooth transition between the cultures.

Exploratory Qualitative Study: Cultural Differences in Student-Teacher Interaction

A small minority of Asian-born females has recently appeared on the faculties of college English communication departments (Forrest Cataldi, Fahimi, and Bradburn, 2005). Do they perceive themselves as lacking credibility when teaching English-speaking American students? How do they establish teacher credibility? Do current cross-cultural theories apply to Asian-born female faculty?

NEW DIRECTIONS FOR TEACHING AND LEARNING • DOI: 10.1002/tl

Method and Participants. I designed a set of interview questions to investigate how Asian-born female faculty establish teacher credibility. The questions were written to elicit narrative answers and allow opportunity for explanation.

Seven Asian-born females whose primary language is other than English were recruited.[1] Six participants had experience teaching English communication-related courses or providing counseling to native English-speaking students in the American Midwest, and one taught in the Southwest. They ranged from adjunct visiting professors to tenure-track and emeritus faculty. Before the interviews I explained the purpose of the study and distributed the interview questions. To protect the participants' identity and promote easy identification during data analysis, pseudonyms were given to each of the seven participants. Four were interviewed in person: Ming Liang, a Taiwanese professor of mass communication; Xiali, a Chinese professor of psychology; Tomoko, a Japanese professor of English; and Fusako, a Japanese counselor. The remaining three participants were interviewed via a series of e-mail exchanges: Ayako, a Japanese professor of communication studies; Hye Young, a Korean counselor; and Hiromi, a Japanese doctoral candidate in communication studies.

Participants were asked a series of questions about (1) the length of their stay and their teaching experience in the United States, (2) their initial concerns about teaching native speakers of English, (3) their perception of credibility acknowledgment by their students, (4) their use of self-disclosure, (5) grade protests by their students of the grades they received, (6) their personal teaching experiences, and (7) strategies they used for effective classroom teaching.

Results and Discussion. I analyzed the interviews according to two thematic categories: teachers' self-perceptions of credibility, and the strategies they developed to connect to their students.

Perceptions of Competency and Teacher Credibility. Participants' responses to the question about initial concerns suggested low self-confidence regarding their own English competency and their knowledge of cross-cultural differences early in their careers. Hye Young, Xiali, Ming Liang, and Ayako stated that they sensed the students had difficulty understanding them even though there were no explicit comments from the students. Hiromi and Xiali received student evaluations stating that they could not understand their instructors because of their accents. Hiromi and Xiali also reported that during class students occasionally asked them to repeat words and sometimes commented that they did not understand the teacher. Ming Liang, who holds a Ph.D. and has two years of teaching experience in the United States, observed the following: "When I saw my students' faces showing confusion during the first few weeks, I was concerned that they had a hard time with my accent. I started using visual aids as much as I could. I then scripted all my lectures, memorized the entire lectures, and rehearsed them before each class."

Ming Liang stated that the students appreciated the visual aids for note-taking purposes, and she felt they helped the students prepare for exams more effectively and efficiently. She also noticed that once the students visually grasped the basic theories and learned the terminology, the auditory explanations and illustrations were more comprehensible to them. Interestingly, the students' confused facial expressions may have been directed to the content of the lecture and not toward their teachers' accents; however, Ming Liang perceived that the language barrier must have caused some level of confusion.

Hye Young, who had three years of counseling experience, confessed that she had a high level of anxiety about communicating in English. She was concerned that because of a lack of proficiency in English she could not make herself understood and thus would be unable to form a rapport with the students. Hiromi, who had three years of teaching experience, and Ayako, who had a doctorate and three years of experience teaching in New Mexico, commented that they were concerned that rather than their students not understanding their English due to their accents, *they* could not understand their students' speech well enough to evaluate them fairly. Ayako noted that her initial concern probably stemmed from her own lack of teaching experience, and from general anxiety and uncertainty about her effectiveness.

Ming Liang, Fusako, Hiromi, and Ayako felt that their students acknowledged their credibility, but Tomoko, with eleven years of teaching experience, and Xiali, with two years of teaching experience, stated that their credibility as teachers was openly challenged. A nonnative English-speaking student in his fifties in Tomoko's class expressed his disappointment with the teacher by saying, "You are too young." Tomoko responded with humor because she did not feel comfortable arguing with him. Likewise, a female student asked if Xiali had a Ph.D. and openly voiced her objection to the teacher's lack of a doctoral degree. Xiali recounted her experience that earlier in her career some students must have sensed her lack of confidence as a teacher and preyed on it. She stated that at first she used the material she was most comfortable with so she could build her confidence and subsequently establish her teacher credibility in class.

Although the participants were confident about their subjects, their perception of language barriers lowered their self-confidence when teaching the material. My experiences during my first few years of teaching parallel many of the stories I heard during the interviews. Once I was openly challenged during the first class session that public speaking should be taught by a native English speaker. I quickly realized that content knowledge was hardly enough to build my credibility as a teacher. In addition to having this content knowledge, I needed to swiftly break the language barrier that my students felt between us.

Strategies for Connecting with Students. During the interviews, three strategies emerged for connecting with students: use of self-disclosure, rapport setting, and elimination of uncertainty. Five participants used some form of self-disclosure to build their credibility. Four stated that they shared their personal experiences in cross-cultural, interpersonal, and professional contexts. They *intentionally* used this strategy, hoping to encourage their students to reciprocate; once the students responded, these participants felt that their disclosures had strengthened their credibility considerably. One participant rated the level of her self-disclosure as moderate and often unintentional, and two stated that they never used or used very few self-disclosures with their students.

All participants shared their approaches to connecting with their students and their efforts to develop rapport early in the course. Hiromi stated that she routinely emphasized the benefits of learning from differences at the beginning. Tomoko described her first writing assignment, personal narrative, as a tool for becoming better acquainted with her students early on. She also employed self-disclosure to stress the importance of cross-cultural sensitivities and individual cultural values.

The most interesting data came from the participants' anecdotes that depicted their cross-cultural experiences. Ayako, Tomoko, and Ming Liang stated that they were at first caught by surprise when their students came to see them in their offices and protested their grades, because they were "not used to it." A female student of mine once claimed that her grade was too low because the assignment had not been graded according to the scale I had promised. When I regraded, her grade was lowered. The student cried for fifteen minutes, accusing me of discrimination.

After experiencing such grade protests, Ayako adapted a strategy to eliminate any uncertainty about grading, and increased students' ability to predict their grades. Similarly, Fusako, who had fifteen years of counseling experience, stated that her most effective approach to connecting with students was to eliminate uncertainty and increase predictability with guidelines for activities and grading.

Ayako also observed the American students' insistence on high grades, while Xiali described her experience and summarized her students as "undisciplined," quoting their unrealistic expectations about receiving leniency on deadlines for personal problems. It is ironic to see these teachers from a high uncertainty avoidance country adapt their cultural practices, such as precise objectives and strict timetables, to satisfy the students of a lower uncertainty avoidance culture.

My experience as a novice teacher overlaps this approach. At first I perceived that American students would prefer more flexible and accommodating classroom management; therefore, deadlines and due dates were not strictly enforced. The students constantly asked what their grades were, how the grades were calculated, and on some occasions, what they could do to raise their grade to A from C during the final week of the semester. After I adopted a point system for grading, along with stricter policies, very few students inquired or protested regarding grades.

NEW DIRECTIONS FOR TEACHING AND LEARNING • DOI: 10.1002/tl

These anecdotes may not be unique to the United States; however, for teachers from Asian countries where the classroom reflects teacher-centered dynamics, such experiences are rather problematic. Just as children are expected to obey their parents at home, students are expected to regard their teachers with respect. In school, the hierarchy between teachers and students is clear. Violation of such social order is unacceptable. Asian teachers who expect a large power distance from students may not be able to tolerate these violations easily. Likewise, students from small-power-distance cultures become equally confused and frustrated when their teachers insist on a power hierarchy in the classroom. This is a recipe for disaster for students and teachers alike.

Hall and Hall's account of high- versus low-context cultures in its paradoxical form (1987) is vividly illustrated in Ming Liang's experience with grade protests. She stated,

> Before receiving his final grade, a male student assumed that he had passed the course with flying colors, and had a party to celebrate. When he received the grade the next day, he realized he had barely passed. He confronted me, saying that he thought he'd receive a high grade because I was "always smiling" and "nice" to him.

Lacking multicultural skills in nonverbal communication, this American student, from a low-context background, relied on his instinct for nonverbal cues. As a result he misinterpreted his teacher's smile as a sign of favoritism toward him when in fact Ming Liang's smile had no specific agenda but represented a natural behavior according to her culture.

It is noteworthy that although all participants in the study shared a high-context cultural background, four participants used an explicit verbal approach (self-disclosure), which is characteristic of a low-context culture, to connect with students from a low-context culture. I too find that explicit communication seems to eliminate students' anxiety toward teachers and classroom practice. I also find that a rapport can be built through listening to the culture stories given by students. Blending my teacher-centered classroom management into the student-centered environment in the United States seems to be the key to providing a successful learning experience for the students.

Although exploratory, these findings provide a foundation for research to fully identify the challenges that Asian-born female faculty face in the English communication classroom. Much information is yet to be gathered in order to examine closely how teacher credibility can be effectively established through the use of the cross-cultural information that is currently available. Future research should question which culture emerges as dominant in a classroom of predominantly English-speaking students when the instructor is an Asian-born female. How do Asian-born female college faculty negotiate the clash of cultures? Can a hybrid culture be created to bridge the communication gap in cross-cultural academic settings?

NEW DIRECTIONS FOR TEACHING AND LEARNING • DOI: 10.1002/tl

Conclusion

In my public speaking class several years ago, an English-speaking American male student commented on his student evaluation sheet that I lectured too much. The evaluation also pointed out that I should design and present the class materials in a manner more enjoyable for the students. The comments also suggested that I give tests and quizzes less often. To date, many of the student evaluation comments from the class with predominantly English-speaking Americans often include their expectation to be entertained and their desire to be less restricted in their study timetable.

Conversely, in my public speaking classes for ESL students, which often consist of students from cultures ranging from Arab, Eastern European, and Asian to Central and South American, the students frequently comment on my preparedness, the manner in which disagreements are handled, and the practice of fairness, along with a polite suggestion that the tests and quizzes should be easier. It seems that my classroom dynamics do reflect in part Hofstede's observations regarding uncertainty avoidance, power distance, and individualism. Interestingly, however, the students in my public speaking classes, regardless of their cultural backgrounds, consistently view a well-organized and highly predictable classroom practice as a positive quality. This positive perception of the class is often simultaneously coupled with the students' perception of the teacher's credibility and competency ("She knows her stuff").

Although instructors' expectations of students are explicitly stated in the course syllabus, students' expectations are rarely communicated to their instructors (Niehoff, Turnley, Sheu, and Yen, 2001). This lack increases students' dissatisfaction with their instructors as well as with the course content. Hendrix (1998) stated that the findings of her study examining the influence of race on teacher credibility indicated that the likelihood of students questioning the credibility of African American teachers depended on the subject matter. This inference seems to parallel the testimonies of Asian-born female instructors obtained in this study. Just as foreign language students expect their teachers to be multicultural and to speak the subject language with a native tongue, English-speaking American students may expect their teachers to be experts in English as well as in American culture. Because student perceptions of instructor effectiveness may be influenced by such factors as the instructor's cultural background and classroom practice, it is important for instructors to tune in to cross-cultural sensitivities and nurture inclusiveness and openness among students.

Note

1. Three participants were my colleagues. Through the Japan-U.S. Communication Association, I e-mailed a request for participation to its members. Two people replied. Finally, my graduate professor at Northeastern Illinois University referred two participants to me.

References

Andersen, J. "Teacher Immediacy as a Predictor of Teaching Effectiveness." In D. Nimmo (ed.), *Communication Yearbook 3.* New Brunswick, N.J.: Transaction Books, 1979.

Forrest Cataldi, E., Fahimi, M., and Bradburn, E. M. *2004 National Study of Postsecondary Faculty (NSOPF: 04) Report on Faculty and Instructional Staff in Fall 2004.* (NCES 2005–172) Washington, D.C.: National Center for Education Statistics, U.S. Department of Education, 2005. Retrieved August 11, 2006, from http://nces.ed.gov/pubsearch.

Frymier, A. B., and Thompson, C. A. "Perceived Teacher Affinity-Seeking in Relation to Perceived Teacher Credibility." *Communication Education,* 1992, *41,* 388–399.

Gorham, J. The Relationship Between Verbal Teacher Immediacy Behaviors and Student Learning." *Communication Education,* 1988, *37,* 40–53.

Hall, E. T. *The Silent Language.* Garden City, N.Y.: Anchor-Doubleday, 1959.

Hall, E. T., and Hall, M. R. *Hidden Differences.* Garden City, N.Y.: Anchor-Doubleday, 1987.

Hendrix, K. "Student Perceptions of the Influence of Race on Professor Credibility. *Journal of Black Studies,* 1998, 28(6), 738–763.

Hofstede, G. *Culture's Consequences: International Differences in Work-Related Values.* Beverly Hills, CA: Sage, 1980.

Hofstede, G. "Cultural Differences in Teaching and Learning." *International Journal of Intercultural Relations,* 1986, *10(3),* 301–320.

Hofstede, G. *Cultures and Organizations.* London: McGraw-Hill International, 1991.

Johnson, S. D., and Miller, A. N. "A Cross-Cultural Study of Immediacy, Credibility, and Learning in the U.S. and Kenya." *Communication Education,* 2002, *51,* 280–292.

McCroskey, J. S. *An Introduction to Communication in the Classroom.* Edina, Minn.: Burgess International, 1992.

McCroskey, J. S., Holdridge, W., and Toomb, J. K. (1974). An instrument for measuring the source credibility of basic speech communication instructors. *Speech Teacher,* 1974, 23, 26–33.

Neuliep, J. W. "A Cross-Cultural Comparison of Teacher Immediacy in American and Japanese College Classrooms. *Communication Research,* 1997, *24,* 431–451.

Niehoff, B. P., Turnley, W. H., Sheu, C., and Yen, H.J.R. "Exploring Cultural Differences in Classroom Expectations of Students from the United States and Taiwan. *Journal of Education for Business,* 2001, 76(5), 289–293.

Teven, J. J., and Hanson, T. L. (2004). The impact of teacher immediacy and perceived caring on teacher competence and trustworthiness. *Communication Quarterly,* 2004, *52,* 39–53.

CHIKAKO AKAMATSU MCLEAN is speech program ESL coordinator and adjunct professor in the Speech and Modern Language Departments at Oakton Community College, Des Plaines, Illinois.

NEW DIRECTIONS FOR TEACHING AND LEARNING • DOI: 10.1002/tl

3

In this chapter, critical race and expectancy violation theories are used to deconstruct students' resistance to a female faculty member of color, a Muslim Arab American who wears the traditional Islamic cover. The author provides a narrative of her teaching experience and some techniques she has used to face such resistance.

From Behind the Veil: Students' Resistance from Different Directions

Ahlam Muhtaseb

My profession as a teacher started when I was a private tutor of Arabic as a foreign language for European white students who worked in my Palestinian city of birth, Hebron. In that context, race was not an issue for me; I had full knowledge authority in this mini educational setting. Race became an issue for me, however, when I moved to the United States in 1998 to pursue my higher education. Since then I have been unveiling the different layers of my racial identity day after day—as a student, as a resident, as a teacher, and so on. My first teaching experience in the United States was also a smooth one. I taught a basic Arabic language class to American students, so my educational authority and credibility were preserved as a result of my racial identity. However, things changed when I started my first teaching assistantship as a doctoral student, teaching public speaking to mainly native speakers of English.

My experience as a female professor of color is different from that of any other colleague, despite the fact that all female faculty of color encounter similar challenges in their teaching experience. I believe that every experience of a female faculty member of color, including mine, is unique. I belong to the group called *sand niggers,* a painful term that reflects the status of Arab and Muslim Americans in the United States. I am an Arab, a Palestinian, and a Muslim female. What adds to my unique experience is the fact that I wear the traditional Islamic female covering, or *hijab.* All of these elements interact to produce my particular experience. This interaction is expressed cleverly by *racial formation theory.* According

to Omi and Winant (1986), the unique experiences of different minorities should be viewed from all of their possible angles. Race is not a fixed, inherited, biological essence; a product of material conditions; or an ideological construct. Historically informed, process-oriented racial formation theory considers race as resulting instead from the critical interaction between historical contingencies, racially defined experiences, and political relationships (Bartlett and Brayboy, 2006). We should therefore analyze race as a system in conjunction with other social factors such as class, gender, nationality, and so forth.

My race, which has been marginalized in the United States, is one of the elements that form my unique experience. The marginalization of Arab Americans, which was well articulated by Abraham (1989, p. 36) as the "political and cultural stigmatization of Arab Americans, and their related subjective experiences," is witnessed in almost all aspects of life in the United States. Abraham traced such discrimination and stigmatization in U.S. society's cultural, social, and political institutions. This marginalization has been increasing and intensifying since 9/11, especially with the ongoing wars in Afghanistan, Iraq, and Palestine.

The role of the media in creating and reinforcing these frames should also be emphasized. According to Domke, Garland, Billeaudeaux, and Hutcheson (2003), audience members commonly accept without challenge the media's representations and framing of different races. Such acceptance results in the public holding stereotypical views of certain minorities, which in turn reinforces a racial hierarchy that benefits whites more than any other group.

Teaching in a white culture is the major challenge I face as a junior faculty member. In this chapter I take a critical race perspective using my personal narratives and experiences to unveil complicated issues in terms of teacher-student interaction. I also use expectancy violation theory to deconstruct my students' initial impressions of and reactions to my racial background, which are based on their previous perceptions of my "in-group." Finally, some suggestions for dealing with tough issues are provided.

Theoretic Underpinnings of Teaching a White Class: Critical Race and Expectancy Violation Theories

From the moment I enter the classroom and students discover that I am the professor, I start the extra-hard work I need to do to survive in a highly diverse teaching environment that ironically is rooted in a conservative white culture. The majority of students on our campus are white, but there is also a large minority of Hispanics, followed by African Americans and Asians. However, whiteness as a social construct is not necessarily color-bound. Actually, it is the whole idea of whiteness as the norm that sets the standards of behavior and expectations in the United States (Williams and Evans-Winters, 2005), thereby affecting my experiences and those of my students. According to critical race theory (CRT), race is a critical factor in

NEW DIRECTIONS FOR TEACHING AND LEARNING • DOI: 10.1002/tl

discussing the experiences of faculty of color. CRT focuses on the importance of providing the white mainstream with alternative narratives by society's marginalized voices (Williams and Evans-Winters, 2005).

Critical Race Theory. CRT, which evolved from oppositional legal scholarship that aimed at fighting racism in the legal system in the mid-1970s, has been applied in the field of education for more than ten years (Bartlett and Brayboy, 2006; Dixson and Rousseau, 2005; Valencia, 2005). This theory has several elements and focuses on issues of racism (in a historical context) combined with gender and class. The five elements associated with CRT are (1) color and gender blindness as a state of denial of racial and gender discrimination; (2) whiteness as property and as the norm; (3) otherness and racial hegemony; (4) social justice and the elimination of sexism, racism, and poverty, among other forms of social injustice; and most important (5) the inclusion of alternative voices of minorities and their oppositional narratives that might differ greatly from those of their white counterparts (Bartlett and Brayboy, 2006; Dixson and Rousseau, 2005; Valencia, 2005).

It is hard to solve a problem when people deny its existence. Many people in the United States, including many of my students, deny any racial and gender inequalities and claim color and gender blindness, as if such blindness would solve the problem of racism and sexism in this country. It is ironic, however, that although these students firmly deny race and gender discrimination, they are usually surprised that their professor is a woman dressed in a way that indicates she is supposed to be "backward and ignorant," similar to Shaheen's conclusion on Arab women's stereotypes (1994), discussed later in the chapter. This is not surprising, because U.S. mainstream media serve as students' main pedagogy in terms of education about the world. Unfortunately the image that the U.S. mainstream media paint of Arabs and Muslims, especially females, is of the uncivilized "other." The effect of such an image on students' expectations of their teachers is also extensively explained by expectancy violation theory.

But before discussing expectancy violation theory, it is crucial to point out another important element of CRT: alternative voices. Valencia (2005, p. 393) explains this issue further by stating that "CRT recognizes the centrality of experiential knowledge of people of color and that such knowledge is valid, appropriate, and essential to understanding, analyzing, and teaching about racism in education." Therefore, in the next section I explore expectancy violation theory using my own "alternative" teaching narratives as a female faculty of color in a white classroom.

Expectancy Violation Theory. Burgoon's expectancy violation theory (1986) states that we evaluate other people on the basis of the stereotypes we have formed, and that we usually evaluate more extremely those who "violate our stereotyped expectations" (Bettencourt and others, 1997; Biernat, Vescio, and Billings, 1999). In the case of Arab Americans, several studies have investigated their portrayal in U.S. mainstream media before September 11, 2001.

Shaheen (1984) documented the negative, dehumanizing stereotypes of Arabs that dominated U.S. television news programming by analyzing a random sample of news segments on television stations such as CBS and NBC during the 1970s and 1980s. In 1994 Shaheen conducted a comprehensive study of the stereotypical depiction of Arabs in comics from the 1950s to the 1990s. He found that 249 of the Arab characters were portrayed as "commoners" and that none was portrayed as a hero or heroine. He also found that Arabs were portrayed mainly as villains, which he sorted into three categories: "the repulsive terrorist, the sinister sheikh, or the rapacious bandit" (1994, p. 123). In particular, Shaheen shed light on the images of Arab women presented in those comics—typically either a faceless housewife or a belly dancer. It was no wonder that when I first arrived in the United States, one of my fellow Fulbrighters, who was European, told me I was a mystery for him because he thought that "women like" me would usually "walk on the side of the road, be very quiet, and rarely talk to foreign men"—a stereotype that was contrary to the way I behaved.

In addition, Shaheen described how the Arab characters in those comics were portrayed using many degrading physical and behavioral features. He warned in particular about the danger that these depictions affected the 150 million young people (including college students) who read these comics weekly, considering that they emphasized negative stereotypes of Arabs and Arab Americans. More recently Shaheen (2001) analyzed nine hundred U.S. Hollywood movies related to Arabs made between 1986 and 2001 and concluded that Arabs were misrepresented in all of the films on the basis of stereotypes found in his earlier research.

Similarly, Lind and Danowski (1998) analyzed the representation of Arabs in U.S. electronic media outlets such as ABC, CNN, PBS, and NPR. They concluded that there was an overwhelming association in the U.S. media between Arabs and violence, threats, and war—constructs that serve to foster stereotypes of Arabs as barbarians, aggressors, and terrorists. In addition, Little (1998) analyzed several books about Arabs written by Western authors and found that in all these books Arabs were portrayed as dirty, lazy, ignorant, superstitious, silly, irrational, cruel, violent, abusive to women, and hating Christians. It is these types of stereotypes that provide the background knowledge for my students about my race, culture, and gender.

In light of all these portrayals of Arabs and Muslims, I usually enter the classroom with the conscious realization that most of my students will hold stereotypes about women like me that are similar to those mentioned by Shaheen and other researchers. This awareness usually makes me a bit uneasy in the first meeting with my students; however, I usually get over that uneasiness after the first meeting. What goes on in the minds of my students is a different story though. To go back to the theory of expectancy violations, sometimes students form their judgments of my qualifications and credibility even before they have the chance to know me or to listen to what

NEW DIRECTIONS FOR TEACHING AND LEARNING • DOI: 10.1002/tl

I have to say. There have been several encounters in which my students have been severe in their judgment of me without giving me the chance to prove to them my professionalism and teaching effectiveness. For example, a student last year decided to drop my class only one day after our first meeting because she thought, according to our department secretary, that my accent was hard to understand.

The expectancy violation theory goes on to state that initial interactions and evaluations are usually based on preconceived stereotypes, but the individual traits of those persons we consider to belong to an out-group ultimately prevail in our judgments and the effect of the stereotypes slowly fades away (Bettencourt and others, 1997). The problem is, however, that the burden of proving individual traits usually falls on the shoulders of faculty members of color when dealing with students' preconceived stereotypes and expectations, whereas their white counterparts can take their privileged position for granted. For example, I go the extra mile to assure my students that I am qualified to teach. I usually tell them that I hold several college degrees, which is another violation of their stereotypical expectations of me. I also make a conscious effort to make my speech clear and understandable despite my accent, although I began learning "proper English" when I was five years old. According to most of my colleagues and former professors, I speak English extremely well. Jackson and Crawley (2003) reached a similar conclusion in their qualitative study of their white students' reactions to the presence and to the pedagogy of black professors. The results of their study indicated that white students were more critical of their black male professors at the beginning of the semester but were more accepting and trusting later on, although the students maintained their conservative views regarding intercultural communication.

To prove my teaching efficiency, I always have a class plan typed out and I present PowerPoint slides of the main points of my lecture. I put my syllabi, lecture notes, assignment instruction sheets, samples of assignments, and grades on the blackboard to make sure there is no room for misunderstanding. I honestly put my heart into teaching. In spite of all my efforts and hard work, I am usually evaluated more negatively than I expect. It is hard for me to compare my evaluations to those received by colleagues with similar experience and rank, but from what I have collected informally, my students' evaluations, especially during the first two years, were lower than those of other assistant professors or even teaching assistants.

This issue of discrepancy in evaluations and judgment has been discussed extensively by Biernat, Vescio, and Billings (1999) in their study of social judgment that employed the expectancy violation theory. They stated that judgment of a favorable in-group member (with perceived good qualities) is usually more positive than that of a favorable out-group member, a process they term *in-group polarization,* which is explained as a means of preserving positive in-group qualities. Because most of my students are either white or normalized to white professors, I usually represent the out-group member or the "other." Several teaching issues reveal the underlying, mostly unconscious in-group favoritism.

One of the problems I sometimes face is the inability to discuss controversial or sensitive topics in class. According to Williams and Evans-Winters (2005), in their reflective study of teaching race-related subjects to instructors, one of the problems they faced was students' focusing on the messenger rather than on the message. This is an issue I definitely deal with whenever I cover issues of race, gender, class, and sexual orientation. A similar conclusion was reached by Jackson and Crawley (2003, p. 217), who contended that "anecdotal data reveal that many White pre-service teachers (and, I suspect, other White non-education students as well) will challenge, debunk, and even question the credentials of faculty of color who discuss these taboo topics. This 'kill the messenger' syndrome may stem from guilt and/or anger at realizing their White privilege and the complicity of their racial counterparts in maintaining a racially stratified system." In my Gender, Race, and Media class it is hard for me to explain inequality of media representation of different segments of society on the basis of gender, class, and race without bringing my own ethnic background to the forefront of the discussion. One of the major challenges for me is to discuss stereotyping.

Many students insist that stereotypes have elements of truth in them. When I try to explain that some stereotypes have nothing to do with facts or statistics and that they are ideologically motivated, socially constructed, and related to the hegemonic narratives of the dominant group in society, students still resist and try to provide examples of stereotypes that are factual. Most of the resistance, not surprisingly, comes from white students, who take the Gender, Race, and Media class with the suspicion that the point of such a class is white bashing. My ethnicity is always on the back burner of any discussion that relates to ethnicity and race. Here are some examples of students' notes in their class evaluations:

> You are very nice. I thought that this course might *revolve around your ethnicity at the beginning of the semester* [emphasis added], but in the end I have to admit that you did a good job keeping this as a non-factor (for the most part).

> Our instructor was always cheerful and pleasant, she made eye contact with us. Asked questions—seemed to treat everyone fairly even though she was from a different country. Instructor had an accent but it did not restrict her use of the English language. She always spoke clearly and did not mind repeating words that were pronounced differently than what we were used to.

> I didn't come to class to listen to the political views of any of my professors. I respect the fact that everyone has the right to have opinions, but a class is not the right time for them.

NEW DIRECTIONS FOR TEACHING AND LEARNING • DOI: 10.1002/tl

Focusing Students on the Message and Not the Messenger of Color

Before the beginning of each quarter I collect the subjective part of previous classes' student evaluations and carefully study them to come up with new teaching strategies. Following are several techniques I have developed to deal with the issue of students' resistance to me in hopes of focusing their attention on the message.

Guest Lecturers. Inviting white guest lecturers to speak about sensitive topics that usually initiate resistance is one of the techniques I use to provide students with an alternative view, which also creates a data mine for me for comparison. For example, last fall I invited a white female journalist to talk about the huge discrepancy between what actually happens between the Palestinians and Israelis and what is shown on U.S. mainstream news channels. To measure students' reactions to the lecturer who spoke on such a controversial issue, I set up an online discussion board for them to use to express their reactions to the lecture for extra credit. Almost all of them admired the speaker and her speech. Here are a couple of the comments I gathered, which can be compared with the above-mentioned student reactions to my overall lecturing.

> I thought her lecture was very informative. It's sad how our society automatically assumes that all Arabs are terrorists, when in reality they are normal people who are willing to open the doors for anyone. They just live in a bad area, and that is what the media is portraying, just the bad things. . . . It was a shock to hear . . . [journalist's name] share her story with our class—to realize that I, along with so many other people have been the passive audience of which we were taught not to be. . . . Her message was a huge awakening for me. [white male student]

I also invited a white female colleague of mine to lecture on the three waves of feminism, and although she was not accepted as the journalist was, she still got many points across to students without the same resistance with which I am usually faced. Last year I also invited a white male colleague who gave an uncontested lecture in my class.

Establishing Credibility. In addition to inviting white professors, I also usually work hard on establishing my credibility. For example, I always share my research projects with my students and even get their feedback. I share with them information I acquire from conferences I attend, and I encourage my students to attend such conferences. Moreover, the most important lesson I have learned is that I always have to be organized and follow my syllabi as much as I can. As a result of this hard work, I usually get high scores in the organization category on students' evaluation forms.

Using Students' Feedback. Finally, taking students' evaluations and comments seriously and analyzing them carefully is very important to understanding the psyche of students. I usually make copies of the evaluations and look at them before I start preparing for the classes I repeat. These evaluations usually help me tremendously to avoid areas of tension that have arisen in previous classes.

Synthesis. Last summer I was in Lebanon collecting Palestinian refugees' narratives of Diaspora when Israel started its thirty-three-day war against Lebanon. After observing U.S. mainstream media coverage, I thought this war would complicate my position as a female faculty of color. The event became another source for the media to use to confirm the stereotypical view of Arabs and violence.

The two theories I have discussed—critical race theory and expectancy violation theory—can help us unveil the problem at hand. We need to understand how students view people like me and what kind of expectations they have of people like me on the basis of what they see, hear, and read in U.S. mainstream media. Identifying and discussing the problem for better understanding is the first step toward a solution. Including this topic of research in our curricula empowers female faculty of color to be voices that bring awareness and understanding. Although I paint a dark picture of my experience as a Muslim Arab American teacher, I hope that the stereotypes of Arab and Muslim Americans will someday evolve into favorable images.

Conclusion

Female faculty of color can, and do, prove their excellence in teaching, professionalism, and knowledge. However, their road is not paved with roses; they actually take more time to achieve what their white, especially male, colleagues achieve. The problem is that sometimes these good, intelligent teachers give up and quit the torturous journey to teaching success. I say torturous because this is how students' harsh evaluations feel to me, especially when my expectations for a good term are high.

In addition to the pain of working hard and being harshly evaluated, a feeling of unfairness makes the experiences of female faculty of color difficult. In this era, most students are not interested in good professors, smart professors, or professional professors; they are interested in beautiful, charismatic, handsome, and most important, entertaining professors. If students learn from the mainstream media that most people are good-looking whites, then their professors should be similar. This image is hard to achieve when you are a female faculty of color.

References

Abraham, N. "Arab-American Marginality: Mythos and Praxis." *Arab Studies Quarterly,* 1989, *11*(2), 17–43.

Bartlett, L., and Brayboy, B. M. "Race and Schooling: Theories and Ethnographies." *Urban Review,* 2006, *37*, 361–374.

Bettencourt, B. A., Dill, K. E., Greathouse, S. A., Charlton, K., and Mulholland, A. "Evaluations of In-Group and Out-Group Members: The Role of Category-Based Expectancy Violation." *Journal of Experimental Social Psychology,* 1997, *33,* 244–275.

Biernat, M., Vescio, T. K., and Billings, L. S. "Black Sheep and Expectancy Violation: Integrating Two Models of Social Judgment." *European Journal of Social Psychology,* 1999, *29,* 523–542.

Burgoon, J. K. "Expectancy Violations: Theory, Research, and Critique." Paper presented at the annual meeting of the Western States Communication Association, Tucson, Arizona, February 1986.

Dixson, A. D., and Rousseau, C. K. "And We Are Still Not Saved: Critical Race Theory in Education Ten Years Later." *Race, Ethnicity, and Education,* 2005, *8,* 7–27.

Domke, D., Garland, P., Billeaudeaux, A., and Hutcheson, J. "Insights into U.S. Racial Hierarchy: Racial Profiling, News Sources, and September 11." *Journal of Communication,* 2003, *53,* 606–623.

Jackson, R. L., and Crawley, R. L. "White Student Confessions About a Black Male Professor: A Cultural Contracts Theory Approach to Intimate Conversations About Race and Worldview." *Journal of Men's Studies,* 2003, *12,* 25–41.

Lind, R., and Danowski, J. "The Representation of Arabs in the U.S. Electronic Media." In Y. R. Kamalipour and T. Carilli (eds.), *Cultural Diversity and the U.S. Media.* Albany: State University of New York Press, 1998.

Little, G. "Representing Arabs: Reliance on the Past." In Y. R. Kamalipour and T. Carilli (eds.), *Cultural Diversity and the U.S. Media.* Albany: State University of New York Press, 1998.

Omi, M., and Winant, H. *Racial Formation in the U.S.: From the 1960s to the 1980s.* New York: Routledge and Kegan Paul, 1986.

Shaheen, J. G. *The TV Arab.* Bowling Green, Ohio: Bowling Green State University Press, 1984.

Shaheen, J. G. "Arab Images in American Comic Books." *Journal of Popular Culture,* 1994, *28,* 123–133.

Shaheen, J. G. *Reel Bad Arabs: How Hollywood Vilifies a People.* Brooklyn, N.Y.: Olive Branch Press, 2001.

Valencia, R. R. "The Mexican American Struggle for Equal Opportunity in Mendez v. Westminster: Helping to Pave the Way for Brown v. Board of Education." *Teachers College Record,* 2005, *107,* 389–423.

Williams, D. G., and Evans-Winters, V. "The Burden of Teaching Teachers: Memoirs of Race Discourse in Teacher Education." *Urban Review,* 2005, *37,* 201–219.

AHLAM MUHTASEB is assistant professor in the Department of Communication Studies at California State University, San Bernardino.

NEW DIRECTIONS FOR TEACHING AND LEARNING • DOI: 10.1002/tl

4

This chapter presents an autoethnography of a Chinese American woman's twenty-five years of experience in higher education at universities in Southern California and the Pacific Northwest. Her career is discussed in four stages: master's teaching assistant and student, part-time instructor, doctoral teaching assistant and student, and professor.

The Permeable and Impermeable Wall of Expectations

Mary Fong

As an undergraduate in the late 1970s and early 1980s, I went to three major universities in Southern California. I did my master's program in California and my doctoral studies in the Pacific Northwest (1989–1994). In my nine years of higher education I had seventy-five teachers. Sixty-one professors were white males, four were nonwhite males—Chinese American, Hawaiian, Egyptian, and Latino—and ten were females—eight whites and two non-whites (Chinese). Scholars have reported that higher education employs a disproportionately low number of faculty of color (Garza, 1993; Tack and Patitu, 1992), which has been my educational experience for almost ten years.

I was one of the few nonwhite undergraduate and graduate students majoring in communication. I was the atypical Asian American daughter who was studying "talking" and could not explain my major to my immigrant parents, who worked long hours in the restaurant business. I was educated primarily as an inner-city Los Angeles (LA) student and lived in Chinatown, LA, for three years. I had no role models. I was an "independent party," with no "buddy" students or faculty mentors to look to. I agree with Plata (1996), who contends that ethnic minority students who arrive on higher education campuses deserve to see and interact with faculty, staff, and administrators of diverse ethnic backgrounds, just as their peers from the dominant culture do.

In this autoethnography, I focus on the difficult and uncivilized students I have encountered. I believe that as a woman of color in higher education, my experiences and the treatment I have received differs from the

expected norm of Caucasian male and acceptable Caucasian female professors. The significance of this argument allows awareness and understanding of women of color in higher education, who have additional struggles with both students and faculty that would not be typical of the expected norm of a professor. These additional struggles bring to light the overlooked discrimination, unfairness, and mistreatment that need to be considered, especially in the evaluation of faculty for tenure and promotion. That is, uninformed misperceptions and unawareness of the sociocultural educational context of female professors of color perpetuates the belief among many decision makers and faculty that no difference exists.

I discuss my teaching experiences of almost twenty-five years in four phases: teaching assistant (TA) at the master's level, part-time instructor, TA at the doctoral level, and tenure-track professor. Within these four phases, I further discuss two components of Collier's presentation of properties on cultural identity (1997): avowal and ascription. *Avowal* refers to a person's presentation of self in demonstrating "who I am" to others in interaction. *Ascription* is concerned with what others perceive and communicate about a person's identity, which may involve stereotypes and attributions.

Master's Teaching Assistant (1982–1983)

As a master's student I was a TA and taught two independent sections of public speaking or small group communication each semester.

Avowal Dimension. The avowal dimension of my cultural identity was apparent in my appearance as an early 1980s atypical college instructor who was Asian American, female, and very young looking.

I did not tell the class that I was a TA. I was not aware of the positive effects of immediacy behaviors, particularly communicating interpersonal closeness and warmth. I presented myself in a straightforward manner, focusing on my goals for each session. I did not have much personality. I intentionally did not smile, because I wanted my students to take me seriously. As a TA I received no training and very little supervision. The TAs were given only the instructor's textbook and manual. We created our own syllabi, assignments, lectures, lesson plans, and so on.

Ascription Dimension. I think my students perceived me as an atypical instructor—a very young, Asian American female teaching public speaking and small group courses.. I do not recall any students writing stereotypical, derogatory comments on my teaching evaluations. For the most part the students were well behaved.

Student Challenge. In my second semester, I had a student who was problematic. He bragged about having a 4.0 grade point average and being a fashion model. He made comparative references to an older Caucasian male professor in order to lessen my credibility.

This problem student gave a demonstration speech on how to pick up girls. I did not require students to have their topics preapproved. The student's presentation included both verbal and nonverbal profanity. I could not believe his inappropriate, tasteless speech. At the end of the week I issued grades to all the students at the close of the session. He received a C– on his speech and was furious. He pointed at me and yelled across the room saying, "I'm going to have you fired!" and stormed outside.

According to Feldmann (2001), the student's disruptive manner was one type of incivility that hinders a "harmonious and cooperative learning atmosphere in the classroom" (p. 137). Disruptive student classroom behaviors are characterized as rebellious, emotional, or escalating. Further, rebellious behaviors tend to be intentional and disrespectful (Hernandez and Fister, 2001).

Within days, the department chair, the student, and I met in my office. The student complained and said, "I'm not going to take this grade. If you don't change it, I'm going to drop the class." I had no intention of changing the grade, especially when a troublemaker would stay in my class to be disruptive. So he dropped my course and I was so pleased.

Part-Time Instructor (1984–1988)

After graduating, I taught part-time at three California State University (CSU) campuses and four city colleges in Southern California. Two of the CSU campuses were diverse and the other campuses' student bodies were predominately Caucasian undergraduates. I also taught at a CSU campus in the South Bay area of LA and in East LA. Students came from the low to upper-middle socioeconomic classes and lived in a very diverse region.

Avowal Dimension. My cultural identity as an instructor had evolved from a serious demeanor to one with personality. I did not have a role model or a mentor. I did not feel confident in my interpersonal skills because of lack of socialization in my upbringing and throughout my college years. I had not experienced being in a leadership role with followers.

Ascription Dimension. My cultural identity as a part-time teacher remained the same as when I was a TA. I was one of two Asian American instructors at a junior college in Orange County. My students, however, were receptive and positive toward me and that made it easy to feel comfortable in the teaching role. My confidence level as a teacher became stronger.

Faculty Challenge. I taught at the junior college in Orange County for almost three years, until a political upheaval forced me out. I was the only part-time, day-time instructor along with a full-time instructor in communication. The college was searching for a new president. There were two candidates: a Caucasian vice president and a Chinese American administrator. The board selected the Chinese American to be the next president of the junior college. I immediately felt repercussions from the decision.

The following semesters my teaching load was reduced from three day-time classes to one evening course to none. There were no grounds for lessening my teaching load to zero. I felt I had no control over my career and destiny.

NEW DIRECTIONS FOR TEACHING AND LEARNING • DOI: 10.1002/tl

Teaching Assistant in a Doctoral Program (1989–1992)

Two years later I made a career move to pursue my doctorate in communication.

Avowal Dimension. As a doctoral TA, the avowal aspect of my cultural identity remained the same as that of the atypical young Chinese American female, but now I was a doctoral student teaching in the Pacific Northwest. The first two quarters of my TAship the students were overall not receptive to me because I did not yet fit the professorial image.

Ascription Dimension. Given my four years of previous teaching experience, I felt confident about my competence as a TA teaching public speaking in a doctoral program. I did not think about my cultural identity as a young female of color teaching as a TA at a major university and how it would affect my students, especially in my first two quarters of teaching. After I sensed an invisible wall between my students and me, and received average teaching evaluations, I began trying to figure out why this was the case.

Student Challenge. The first quarter I taught public speaking, almost all of the students were Caucasian males. There were five female students. One student was an African American male and one a Korean American female. I noticed that the students did not laugh at my jokes as had the students I taught in Southern California. These students did not participate much. I felt an invisible wall between them and me. Reflecting on the second quarter of teaching, I recalled four students who were impolite in class. There were also two male students who had an attitude and two female students who giggled and chatted in class.

One white male student came to class late several times; one time he walked directly and closely in front of me as I was conducting class. Another white male student rolled his eyes and yawned widely without covering his mouth almost every class session. He came to my desk after class and said, "I think the student speeches are boring. I graduated as the valedictorian of my high school class." I said, "Oh, really. Well, they are beginning speakers. I thought some of them gave good speeches. I look forward to hearing your speech."

The student did an excellent job. On his speech evaluation he received an A. However, on the flip side of the evaluation form I wrote a note to him. I essentially said that he might think he was the cream of the crop, but when it came down to the top two or three candidates being considered for a job, the interviewers will sense the candidate's character, respectfulness, humbleness, collegiality, and so on. I intentionally wrote the note on the back of his A evaluation form so that if he did not like what I had written and crumpled up the form, he would be crumpling up his A.

By the third quarter of teaching I knew that my TA position was in jeopardy. I needed to penetrate the invisible wall I sensed being put up by many of my students. This invisible wall of student expectations was an

NEW DIRECTIONS FOR TEACHING AND LEARNING • DOI: 10.1002/tl

image of the model "professor." In an attempt to penetrate the invisible wall, I required my students to come to my office hours after they had received their first evaluation. This time enabled me to talk personally with my students about their evaluations and their next speech topic, and to praise and encourage them.

I did not sense an invisible wall that quarter. The class was fairly balanced between male and female students. There were a few nonwhite students in class. I did not teach the course any differently than I did the first two quarters. That third quarter, however, my teaching evaluations were in the high 4's.

Faculty Challenge. My second quarter was under way when the results of my teaching evaluations from the first quarter were available. On a five-point scale I received 3.5s on the average. The department chair threatened not to renew my TA position for the following year. I told her that I had taught this course successfully many times in California, to the point that I did not have to prepare much. She then blamed me for not being prepared for class and said that was why I was not getting the scores she wanted.

I left her office feeling offended, misunderstood, and confused about why I was in such a predicament. As I reflected on both teaching quarters, I came to a realization. In the first quarter there was a high percentage of white males in class, a handful of women, and only two minorities. I figured that I had not met the students' expectations of the model image of a professor who was a white, middle-aged male. Instead I walked through the classroom door as the atypical college instructor—a young, female, Asian American doctoral student.

What made matters worse was that the department chair was not supportive of my teaching evaluation results after the second quarter. She made comments like, "It was a fluke that you got the research assistantship" and "It was a fluke that you got high teaching evaluations midway through the third quarter."

The following quarter she reassigned me to assist two professors in their mass lecture halls. I told her I could not accept this assignment because I was preparing to take my comprehensive exams. I knew it would be much more work to assist two professors. The Caucasian department chair said, "If you don't take it, then you can forget about receiving anymore funding from this department in the future." Without a TA position I would receive no out-of-state tuition and no monthly stipend. I felt victimized and accused of "bad" teaching. I chose not to be a TA and applied for in-state residency and was able to pay in-state tuition the remaining quarters of my doctoral studies.

Professor (1992 to Present)

I accepted a tenure-track assistant professor position in the Inland Empire, sixty miles northeast of LA. Less than six months after the LA police were found not guilty in the beating of Rodney King, the South LA riots occurred. Racial tension was in the air. The Inland Empire is known to house conservative, low- to middle-income Caucasians and minorities.

NEW DIRECTIONS FOR TEACHING AND LEARNING • DOI: 10.1002/tl

An article in the local *Sun* newspaper dated April 30, 2006 ("Grad Rate in Dire State"), reported on a Manhattan Institute study that examined the nation's one hundred largest urban school districts. The particular school district in the Inland Empire was ranked last at 42 percent. This means that four in ten students graduate from this school district. Today, the northeast region of the Inland Empire has flourished in terms of new track homes and businesses. However, the educational system still needs improvement. The university in the Inland Empire is designated a Hispanic-serving institution that has a diverse student body. Many students are first generation and college-bound from low socioeconomic backgrounds.

Avowal Dimension. My identity as an assistant professor included being new at this institution, having all-but-dissertation status, and being the only Asian American female professor in the College of Arts and Letters for the first three years. I had never encountered a class of students in Southern California who displayed blatant incivility toward me, until I arrived here. There was a different culture of students in this inland region.

Ascription Dimension. I believe that my students viewed me as a new, young-looking Asian female professor, a rarity at the university. I think my students thought I was an inexperience teacher. For these reasons, they saw me as not fitting the professorial image.

Student Challenges. In the fall of 1992 I walked into my first inter-cultural course. Before I said one word a Caucasian female student in her late twenties (who had two children) sitting in the front row emitted negative energy just by immediately folding her arms, crossing her legs, turning her head, and staring out the window the entire class period. I simply ignored her.

The following week an Italian American student walked into class and said angrily, "You just don't understand us." I said, "What is it that you think I don't understand?" She said, "You just don't understand us." She turned around and sat down at her desk. A few weeks later I saw this same student in the supermarket. After I said hello three times, she finally said hi with a gruff voice and no eye contact.

Throughout the quarter I caught glimpses of bitter expressions from a divorced student in her forties. Another student, after receiving the hand-out for the first assignment, said loudly, "This looks like a stupid assignment!" I looked at her and then ignored her. I wished I was having a nightmare so that I could just wake up and shake it off but unfortunately it was reality.

I sensed that because the students in my intercultural class perceived me to be a very young Asian female new to teaching at this college they had stereotyped me as a person who had had a smooth life, having jumped through all the hoops with expediency and no problems. Even one of my colleagues in my first year said to me with a serious expression, "You look young. You really do look young."

NEW DIRECTIONS FOR TEACHING AND LEARNING • DOI: 10.1002/tl

At the end of my first quarter of teaching, a middle-aged Caucasian female undergraduate who respected me, and who eventually graduated from medical school, wrote a letter to the department chair in which she said:

> From the first week of class . . . she was interrupted, challenged. . . . After Ms. Fong left the room, I heard comments like, "We'll fix her" and "Let's see how she likes getting an F." I suppose there are students in every class who take out their own poor attitude and inadequacies on the instructors' evaluation. I would hope that those obviously "problem" students who write out a hasty negative comment will be seen for what they are and that good instructors are not being hurt in any way by spur-of-the-moment comments.

In the following quarter I had two female African American and Middle Eastern students who were basketball players in my intercultural course. In class we had a week of discussion on African American culture. The African American basketball player did not show up for the second session of discussion. That same week the acting department chair told me that the African American student had come to complain about the articles. The acting department chair said, "Just pull the articles. You don't want to have conflict in your class. She said that she would call the NAACP."

During that quarter I also noticed that both of the basketball players would go into a Caucasian, middle-aged male faculty member's office. My colleague's office is kitty-corner from my office. Once I overheard him asking them, "So how was she today?" as he was closing his door. One student said, "Oh, she's like a girl" and the door shut. On the last day of class another student came by my office to forewarn me that two basketball players were circulating a petition to try to get me fired. Not once did they come to talk with me about their concerns. No other students signed the petition.

In my third year of teaching intercultural communication, two African American students felt that I was treating African Americans on a group assignment differently from other cultural groups. In the assignment instructions I had encouraged students to interview someone from an ethnic group who was either first or second generation so that the interview would be culturally insightful. By the third generation, many ethnic group members become Americanized. African Americans often do not know what generation they are; therefore, a student interviewing an African American would not need to be concerned about whether the person interviewed was first or second generation. The two black students continued to refute me, saying that I was treating African Americans differently from other ethnic groups.

Both students complained to the department chair, and the conservative, middle-aged, Caucasian male chair had had them in his class and liked both students. He never talked to me about the incident nor did he have a conference with all of us. I believe that the department chair sided with the students because of his prejudice toward me and his lack of understanding of my intent and of the situation.

The department chair gave me an unfair faculty evaluation when I applied for tenure and promotion, stating that I was "not open-minded," even though no student comments to that effect appeared on any of my teaching evaluations. He also gave me no credit for having three top convention papers, and he counted one less journal article than I had published. I received only tenure that year. I complained to the department chair about his unfair and incomplete evaluation of me and pointed out several mistakes. The following year he wrote a fair and accurate evaluation, and I received promotion to associate professor. Both Caucasian male faculty are no longer in the department.

Discussion

On the basis of my six years of TA and part-time teaching in the 1980s, I found students in metropolitan Southern California (that is, Los Angeles, Long Beach, Irvine, and South Bay) to be receptive to a young female professor of color. I think their receptivity was in part due to living in a diverse region. With the exception of Irvine, the other colleges I worked at during this time consisted of diverse students and communities. Today Irvine is diverse. When I was a TA at Long Beach I had only one unfavorable student, who had an ego and an arrogant disposition.

In the 1990s I experienced the most unfavorable student and faculty challenges at the universities in the Inland Empire and the Pacific Northwest. During that era both locations had a predominantly Caucasian student population and community. Diversity in the classroom was lacking. Students were from low- to middle-class socioeconomic backgrounds. The disruptive students in five of my classes in the Inland Empire have been Caucasians, African Americans (one athlete), and one Middle Eastern student athlete. One of the three classes I taught as TA in a doctoral program in the Pacific Northwest consisted of mostly Caucasian males who were reserved and did not appreciate my sense of humor, whereas the California students were receptive to me, especially when I was a part-time instructor. The second class I taught as a doctoral TA was predominately Caucasian with a balance of males and females. A handful of students were arrogant, rude, or nonparticipatory. In two classes I sensed an impermeable invisible wall of expectations of the professorial image. The incivility I experienced in this region was rudeness (continuous yawning, chattiness, giggling, tardiness, and so on).

I experienced the most student incivility in my teaching career in the Inland Empire. I would like to emphasize that the majority of my teaching experience here has been positive. However, in my initial years, a noticeable number of students displayed character problems (such as egotism, arrogance, argumentativeness, jealousy, insecurities, control issues, and power abuse) and have chosen uncivil behavior. Further, students who have character problems are prone to choose to act with incivility when they perceive

NEW DIRECTIONS FOR TEACHING AND LEARNING • DOI: 10.1002/tl

a "vulnerable" instructor (such as one who is female, young, nonwhite, and new on campus). The student incivility I have experienced has involved power struggles: unproductive arguing, maintaining a negative attitude, negative outbursts, going to another faculty member to complain, trying to undermine the teacher's position or authority, and so on.

In some institutions of higher education in which the student body and faculty are not diverse, I have had problems with discrimination and mistreatment, such as at Irvine, in the Pacific Northwest, and in the Inland Empire—regions that at the time were not diverse. However, this does not necessarily mean that diversity makes an institution discrimination free. I recently have seen blatant mistreatment and discrimination by Caucasian faculty toward nonwhites, and even by a Latino male against a Latina. I have experienced faculty in positions of power who either were inflexible or discriminatory, or who lacked understanding of situations. As a result some faculty in positions of power made inaccurate assumptions and decisions that were unfair and damaging.

The incivility of students in the Inland Empire has lessened considerably for me. I believe that such incivility has lessened because my youthful appearance and seeming newness are no longer matters of contention. Also, the student body and faculty are increasingly diverse in terms of ethnicity and gender. However, student incivility has not been entirely eradicated. Last quarter one TA, whom I trained and supervised, tried to undermine me.

This autoethnography has shown that both student and faculty challenges have occurred because I have been discriminated against for being young, female, and of color—not the typical professorial image. As a result, some student evaluations of my teaching performance have been inaccurate and unfair. Further, faculty in decision-making positions regarding faculty retention and promotion who are unaware or insensitive or who lack understanding of the difficulties and complexities that confront a female professor of color have had a tendency to make unjust evaluations and decisions. Institutions of higher education need to be informed and to act fairly, appropriately, and ethically in response to these concerns.

I believe that mentorship is necessary for incoming women of color in higher education because of the multiplicity of stresses they encounter. A mentor would help provide support and advice that could make a difference in retaining and helping these women professors of color to achieve success in higher education.

References

Collier, M. J. "Cultural Identity and Intercultural Communication." In L. Samovar and R. Porter (eds.), *Intercultural Communication: A Reader.* Belmont, Calif.: Wadsworth, 1997.

Feldmann, L. J. "Classroom Civility Is Another of Our Instructor Responsibilities. *College Teaching,* 2001, 49(4), 137–140.

Garza, H. "Second-Class Academics: Chicano/Latino Faculty in the U.S. Universities." *New Directions in Learning,* 1993, 53, 33–41.

"Grad Rate in Dire State." *San Bernardino County Sun,* Apr. 30, 2006, pp. 1, A8.
Hernandez, T. J., and Fister, D. L. "Dealing with Disruptive and Emotional College Students: A Systems Model." *Journal of College Counseling,* 2001, *4(1),* 49–62.
Plata, M. "Retaining Ethnic Minority Faculty at Institutions of Higher Education." *Journal of Instructional Psychology,* 1996, 23(3), 221–228.
Tack, M. W., and Patitu, C. L. "Faculty Job Satisfaction: Women and Minorities in Peril." Washington, D.C.: George Washington University, School of Education and Human Development, 1992. (ED 355859)

MARY FONG *is a full professor in communication at California State University, San Bernardino, and has published extensively.*

NEW DIRECTIONS FOR TEACHING AND LEARNING • DOI: 10.1002/tl

5

Race matters in the classroom when you are a minority female faculty member. This chapter discusses the emergence of the adaptive female academic of color who, while teaching in several countries, balances a happy work and family life.

You Can't "De-Race" and "De-Womanize" Me: Experiences When You Go Global

Aparna G. Hebbani

An East Indian woman, a wife, a graduate student, a mother, a doctoral student, a graduate teaching assistant of color, a divorcee with a child, a doctoral candidate, and finally an assistant professor—this was my identity as I progressed through academia.

I am now a wife, a mother of two kids, a homemaker with a doctorate, and a casual lecturer in Australia. This is my identity now. In this chapter I describe my experiences as a female faculty member of color teaching in Australia, Malaysia, and Hong Kong. After several years of researching the minority professor's perspective in the classroom, my conclusion is that I will always be assessed on the basis of assumptions made about me because I am a minority female academic.

Experiences Teaching Internationally

In 2004 I moved with my family to Australia from the United States because my husband got a promotion. The offer was too lucrative to pass up, so I quit my job as a tenure-track assistant professor and relocated. This decision I have never regretted, but there have been consequences.

Experiences Down Under. After moving to Australia I taught organizational behavior courses for a graduate school of business, both onsite and offshore (in Malaysia and Hong Kong). My classes each semester comprised

NEW DIRECTIONS FOR TEACHING AND LEARNING, no. 110, Summer 2007 © Wiley Periodicals, Inc.
Published online in Wiley InterScience (www.interscience.wiley.com) • DOI: 10.1002/tl.273

45

approximately sixty MBA students, most of whom would fit the *nontraditional student* category (that is, in the age group thirty to fifty, working full-time, and studying part-time), with a few international students in the *traditional student* category (that is, in the age group twenty to thirty, working part-time, and studying full-time). Statistics provided by the school administrators reveal that out of the approximately eighteen hundred students, twelve hundred were male and six hundred were female. There were eight full-time faculty and twenty-two casual faculty, including myself.[1]

These statistics show that a third of the enrolled students were women working full-time. In informal discussions with these women, I learned that most of them had family commitments and worked an eight-to-five job. It made sense, then, that they were always keen for me to talk about the female perspective on balancing work and family life. The next section presents research conducted in Australia about the experiences of female students, laying the foundation for where these women were coming from.

The Australian Education System. As a first-world country, Australia faces issues similar to those faced by any other first-world country, such as the United States. The Karpin Report (Karpin, 1995) found that the glass ceiling in corporate Australia (that is, there were more males than females in senior levels) appeared to be thickening, and it recommended that management education in Australia increase female enrollment and raise gender awareness in the classroom. These findings are supported by other research (Tancred, 1997; White, 2001).

Although literature has shown that in Australia the majority of management education and training is still male centered (Smith, 2000), I have witnessed more female students in my courses than males. In addition to the documented promotion of masculinity in higher education, the literature also illustrates that women in education have a tougher time balancing school with work and family responsibilities. In Australia it is women who take primary responsibility for family care. They often take longer to complete their tertiary studies than male students, who are less likely to have their studies interrupted by pregnancy and child care (Bessant, 2004). Addressing gender in the classroom and specifically in management education also seems to be more important, if not more pertinent, to women than to men. Students might be selected according to whether or not the relevant academic advisor or research office believes there is a good chance they will complete a doctorate in four years or a research master's in two years, and "this disadvantages those people who are likely to need more time to complete their program because of factors like family and childcare responsibilities" (Bessant, 2004, p. 2).

This experience is common to many Australian women who want to study while working but get less support from their employers than men do. Dean (1998) and the 2001 Australian Senate Committee Report (Parliament of Australia Senate, Employment, Workplace Relations and Education

NEW DIRECTIONS FOR TEACHING AND LEARNING • DOI: 10.1002/tl

Committee, 2001) observed that in Australia "men are more likely to be given time off to study, and are more likely to have their fees paid by employers because women are less likely to have uninterrupted and secure employment than men" (Bessant, 2004, p. 2).

Question for Introspection. Given that women have a tougher time getting through the higher education system in Australia, one question posed to me by female students was, "Are you *happy*? You have had to give up a stable job where you were very happy. To sacrifice that must not have been easy." Finding the answer to their question was not easy. Research has shown that in Australia, life context factors such as marriage, family, and prevalent sociocultural values influence women's career paths and constrain actual career and salary opportunities (Poole and Langan-Fox, 1997). Where my female students were coming from was that I had managed to get a doctorate and a good university job while raising children and being a happy family, only to quit a full-time job and work part-time.

I was a casual lecturer, but with young children at home I was actually working full-time trying to fulfill both tasks to the best of my ability. In short, I was the primary caretaker of my children while working full-time. Being a female in academia, I had adapted and taken up temporary work so I could spend more time taking care of my family. With my husband mostly away, life was hectic. According to Hakim (2003, p. 57):

> Adaptive women prefer to combine employment and family work without giving a fixed priority to either. They want to enjoy the best of both worlds. Adaptive women are generally the largest group among women, and will be found in substantial numbers in most occupations. Certain occupations, such as school teaching, are attractive to women because they facilitate an even work-family balance—and it is not easy. The great majority of women who transfer to part-time work after they have children are adaptive women who seek to devote as much time and effort to their family work as to their jobs. For example, seasonal jobs, temporary work, or school-term jobs all offer a better work-family balance than the typical full-time job, especially if commuting is involved. For lack of a better solution, adaptive women sometimes take ordinary full-time jobs.

In Australia, academics at the senior levels generally have a doctoral degree (Hopkins, 2004), but in my case I was the only part-time lecturer with a doctorate, although there were several tenured full-time lecturers above me without doctorates. The requirement of having a doctorate may be a barrier to women if they have or are planning to have children. The doctoral requirement, along with a good publication record, means that moving up the ladder in academia is a challenging path for a working mother. As White (2000, p. 49) says, "At one level surviving and advancing in the professoriate is linked in part to early career choices. These include whether or not one plans an academic career; tries to juggle full-time teaching with

New Directions for Teaching and Learning • DOI: 10.1002/tl

postgraduate study; chooses to complete a Ph.D. before embarking on an academic career; chooses to do a postdoctoral fellowship before becoming an academic; chooses to have children; and chooses to focus on teaching or research or both."

Teaching in Australia has been an enriching experience. The next section discusses my experiences teaching in Malaysia and Hong Kong. This experience added to my repertoire of multiple identities as a female of color in academia.

Offshore Teaching.   Australian universities are cashing in on the lucrative offshore education industry. According to Pearson (2004, p. 20):

> Australian universities and other higher-education establishments rely heavily on income from fee-paying international students, who made up 23 percent of the country's 930,000 higher-education students last year [2003], according to government figures. Most of the country's 39 universities, keen to win a share of an education export industry worth some $4 billion in all sectors, have scrambled to set up offshore campuses in recent years. Academics say some have cut corners in doing so.

I taught for my university's offshore programs in Malaysia and Hong Kong. I went to Malaysia to do some intensive teaching over three days (then a local lecturer taught the rest of the course).[2] Full-time faculty were not keen on taking up such teaching in addition to their regular teaching load, because they had already done it before. This proved to be a learning experience for me and an opportunity to visit new places!

Experiences in Malaysia.   Indians came to Malaysia more than a century ago as cheap labor to help build roads and railways, and to work on rubber plantations. In 1990 there were 1.4 million ethnic Indians in Malaysia—8 percent of the total Malaysian population—of whom 85 percent were Tamils (Aznam, 1990a). The uniqueness of this Indian community is that although they look Indian and follow the Indian customs and traditions followed by their forefathers who left India centuries earlier, most of them have never been to India. As one Indian said, "My children might want to visit India as a tourist, but they would hardly consider it going home" (Aznam, 1990b, p. 16). The second generation has loosened ties with the motherland and considers Malaysia to be their homeland. This Indian population has a distinct Malaysian identity (that is, they speak a purer form of the South Indian language, Tamil, compared to the language spoken nowadays in India).

I arrived in Kuala Lumpur determined to make the most of this intercultural experience. The Indian taxi driver assumed that I knew Tamil because I was Indian; he started a conversation in Tamil, and I understood nothing! To my surprise, some hotel employees of Indian origin gave me "the look," which is hard to describe in words but the reader can identify this look as acknowledging that I was one of them. It also turned out that the local lecturer was also of Indian origin but had never visited India. As I walked into class on the first day, I was caught off guard by a sea of students who looked like me. Of the forty students enrolled, 95 percent were of Indian origin with Indian names. In the past, my students have *not* looked like me but have been Caucasian, African American, or Asian (such as of Chinese origin), give or take one or two Indians. The numbers were flipped around this time.

Question for Introspection. During the first class break, most of the students talked to me about how happy they were to be taught by an *Indian* female with a doctorate who was now teaching for an Australian University. I have purposely added emphasis to the word *Indian* because this is what they chose to see me as. None of them had visited India, but they were more Indian than me, stuck in a time warp where the Indian culture they knew was still very orthodox and out of touch with the India of today. They could not comprehend a modern India corrupted by Western culture. Another unique question was posed to me, but for you to make sense of it, I need to lay the groundwork.

Most Malaysian Indians I met during my stay were quite dark in complexion, perhaps due to the tropical weather. One female student commented that I was the fairest Indian she had ever seen! Were Indians in India this fair? Over the next few days, during breaks and during vegetarian lunches in my honor, I was conducting classes on India in the twenty-first century to bring my students up-to-date on the India of today. I ended up having a wonderful experience in which I learned a lot about who I was and how the term *Indian* can refer to different types of Indians depending on where you lived and when your ancestors migrated from India.

Interestingly, the Indian taxi driver taking me back to the airport for my return flight to Australia asked me about my background and was taken aback that a wife and mother of two children had the audacity to leave her family and travel abroad for work. How unthinkable and criminal this act was! How could my husband let me do this? I did not fit his mold of a good Indian married woman (even though I was an academic and he was a taxi driver).

From Malaysia, we now move on to my experiences teaching in Hong Kong.

Experiences in Hong Kong. I taught in Hong Kong several times on trips lasting two weeks.[3] Hong Kong was a vibrant city that seemed quite crowded with locals (Hong Kong Chinese), mainland Chinese (I could not tell the difference), expatriates (Caucasians), and tourists.

In this city of approximately six million, a range of conflicting viewpoints and emotions can be found with regard to foreigners, non-Chinese, and mainland Chinese. Lilley (2001) states that intolerance and racism are pervasive in society and permeate the classroom. In Lilley's experience, students flatly denied the existence of racism or ethnic tensions in Hong Kong:

NEW DIRECTIONS FOR TEACHING AND LEARNING • DOI: 10.1002/tl

It is precisely in the small exchange of everyday interactions that those who are not Hong Kong Chinese are made to feel inferior. Aggressive, overtly racial abuse or violence is relatively unknown. Rather, Indian executives find it difficult to rent a flat, even when their family has resided in Hong Kong for generations; Black Americans are rejected for English teaching positions because employers state they want someone with blond hair and blue eyes; Black Africans find that taxis will not stop for them. [p. 129]

In my classes, most of the males were in high positions with multinational corporations while females were trying to climb the corporate ladder. My female students also said that most females in Hong Kong marry late, because the cost of living is quite high, and choose not to have children for the same reason. Most males in my class were married with children and domestic servants, and most females were either unmarried or had no children.

I never experienced the explicit racism or ethnic tension noted by Lilley. If anything, the Chinese students showed more respect toward me as an educated person. However, I did hear racist remarks about the mainland Chinese and was warned to be cautious of them. Such behavior is greatly influenced by collectivism and high-power distance (Hofstede, 1991), situational orientation (Hsu, 1981), saving face, and insider-outsider distinctions (Hsu, 1981). According to Du-Babcock and Babcock (1996, p. 82), "The Chinese respect for authority (high-power orientation) and respect for the teacher as a symbol of this authority reinforces this opportunity. However, as an instructor shows an understanding of the Hong Kong environment during the semester, the instructor moves towards becoming an insider and consequently being judged by different criteria." A perception also exists that Western academics are better at teaching business than local Chinese academics (Bennington and Xu, 2001). During every visit, students would make great efforts to pool money to buy me an end-of-the-course gift (such as traditional mooncakes) or take me to a lavish buffet meal at an upscale Buddhist vegetarian restaurant. Keen to learn about the local culture, I never lost an opportunity to venture outside the traditional tourist spots.

Question for Introspection. Given that my experiences teaching in Malaysia and Hong Kong were quite different from my experiences teaching in Australia, why did it seem that I might have been more of a novelty to my students in the two Asian cultures? In Malaysia my students were more curious about me being a "true" female Indian academic. Students treated me with respect tinged with curiosity, which stems from their cultural upbringing (especially saving face). Not only did I make an impact on my students (being an international female academic), but in turn they enriched my experiences as well. It was simply wonderful teaching students from my own cultural background, something I had not experienced before. Teaching in Hong Kong was being at ease in an eastern culture, where the teacher was respected and looked up to. I now realize that one commonality among my experiences, regardless of the country, was that I was a *female* academic.

NEW DIRECTIONS FOR TEACHING AND LEARNING • DOI: 10.1002/tl

Discussion

My husband took another giant leap up the corporate ladder. We had to move to another city within Australia. Now it was *his* turn to travel overseas while I became a homemaker and again put my career on the back burner. Writing this chapter resulted in increased questioning and speculation about my own identity. Teaching internationally has made me what I call a "vagabond academic," a female academic of color with a shifting identity of "international" professor.

The Adaptive Female Academic?

Coming back to the core issue of this chapter—why was I such a novelty to my female students? I was a woman with a doctorate and a happy but hectic family life. Interestingly, my Aussie students did not place any importance on the noticeable fact that I was also a minority, perhaps because Australia is a comparatively egalitarian society. My Aussie female students instead chose to hone in on my being a female academic. Even though more than half of the staff employed in Australian universities are women, like me they are employed as general staff. According to Bessant (2004, p. 2), "Although there have been some gains for women academics over the past two decades—in 1985 they represented one-fifth of all academics; eighteen years later they account for two-fifths of the academic workforce—with fewer postgraduate students coming through the ranks, it is likely that there will be fewer women entering academia."

This finding is supported by White (2003, p. 46), who says that "academic women in senior levels in Australian universities have not reached a critical mass despite equity programmes in universities for several decades." The statistics say it all, with "5 men for every woman (full-professor level), 2 males to every female (senior lecturer level) and women in majority at the lecturer level" (Maslen, 2003, p. 30).

Research Agenda: Should I Publish or Perish? I was happy balancing work and family life, but this came at a cost. I did not have the time or opportunity to build on my research agenda, and I had no funding to travel to conferences. I was not alone, because according to White (2003, p. 48), given the high number of female academics at the lecturer level, "many have greater teaching and administrative loads and fewer opportunities to conduct research." White (2003, p. 50) sums it up by saying that in Australia "women are excluded from 'the boys club' in subtle ways. Some women do get promoted, but often they pay a price." Juggling the demands of home and office is tough for women; this is perhaps why Australian women do not seek promotions to senior positions within academia (Maslen, 2003).

It all comes back to the choices and decisions we make. Research took a backseat in my life as I focused on teaching and spending quality time with my family when I could have had a career on the research track, with limited time to spend with my children. To my Australian female students it mattered not that I was an Indian American living in Australia but that I was a woman who had a doctorate, a good job, and a happy family life. To my female students in Malaysia and Hong Kong, it did matter that I was an Indian American living in Australia, and that I was a woman who had a doctorate, a good job, and a happy family life.

Synthesis. Wherever I teach I will always be a female of color. The point here is that as a female minority academic, I am still a rarity (hence this chapter). Whether I am in the United States, Australia, Malaysia, or Hong Kong, I am still a rarity. One day this will change. Being a female academic has not been easy. As a female minority academic with young children and a happy family (note that "minority academic" and "woman with a happy family" are two separate entities), I do have it all. I am the primary caregiver for my children while many male academics have the benefit of not having to worry about that at all. I now teach online and am immediately recognized as a minority because of my name, but I am still mistaken to be male (I have not displayed my photograph in the staff information section). The fact remains that I am not male and I am not white—hence the title of this chapter. As long as I do not fit this norm, I will remain a novelty.

Conclusion

We all seek to make sense of the world we live in on the basis of our experiences. Sometimes, we build on these experiences to enrich our lives; other times we choose to ignore them. We continue to build and rebuild our worldview. The students I taught had a different worldview depending on where they were geographically. As a result, some chose to focus on my being female while others emphasized my being a female of color in the classroom. These varied experiences have shaped my worldview and self-identity. Regardless of what position I hold or what sort of family I have, one fact is certain: I (and others like me) will always be assessed as female faculty of color. Balancing work and family life is a struggle and I am not trying to downplay the implications that come with it. I have a happy relationship, and my premise is that if you are happy on the home front, you just might be less stressed at work, and thereby achieve a happy work-family balance. It is up to us to find that happy medium, wherever it might be.

Notes

1. In Australia, the term *casual faculty* means a non-tenure-track part-time worker (that is, an adjunct instructor).

2. Assignments were graded by this person (under my supervision) and I graded the exam.

3. I did all the teaching in intensive blocks and then came back to Australia. Completed assignments were then mailed to me for grading.

NEW DIRECTIONS FOR TEACHING AND LEARNING • DOI: 10.1002/tl

References

Aznam, S. "Malaysia: The Forgotten Ones." *Far Eastern Economic Review*, 1990a, *148*(23), 15.

Aznam, S. (1990b, June 7). Ethnic Indians see Malaysia as Home: New Motherland. *Far Eastern Economic Review*, 1990b, *148*(23), 16.

Bennington, L., and Xu, L. "Relative Benefits of Offshore MBA Study: An Australia–China Twinning Model." *Journal of Higher Education Policy and Management*, 2001, *23*(2), 219–230.

Bessant, J. "Equity and the Impact of the Nelson Reforms: Gender Equity Has No Place in the Latest Restructure of Higher Education." *Arena Magazine*, 2004, *73*, 23–24.

Dean, A. "Why Having a Family Is Still a Bad Career Move." *The Bulletin*, November 17, 1998, pp. 22–23.

Du-Babcock, B., and Babcock, R. "Patterns of Expatriate-Local Personnel Communication in Multinational Corporations." *Journal of Business Communication*, 1996, *33*(2), 141–164.

Hakim, C. "Competing Family Models, Competing Social Policies." *Family Matters*, 2003, *64*(3), 52–62.

Hofstede, G. *Cultures and Organizations: Software of the Mind—Intercultural Cooperation and Its Importance for Survival.* Berkshire, U.K.: McGraw-Hill, 1991.

Hopkins, S. "Women in Economics Departments in Australian Universities: Is There Still a Gender Imbalance?" *Economic Papers: Economic Society of Australia*, 2004, *23*, 201–211.

Hsu, F. *American and Chinese Passage to Differences.* (3rd ed.) Honolulu: University of Hawaii Press, 1981.

Karpin, D. (Chair). *Enterprising Nation: Renewing Australia's Managers to Meet the Challenges of the Asia-Pacific Century.* Report of the Industry Task Force on Leadership and Management Skills. Canberra: Australian Government Publishing Service, 1995.

Lilley, R. "Teaching Elsewhere: Anthropological Pedagogy, Racism and Indifference in a Hong Kong Classroom." *Australian Journal of Anthropology*, 2001, *12*, 127.

Maslen, G. "Through the Class Ceiling." *The Bulletin with Newsweek*, 2003, *121*, 28–32.

Parliament of Australia Senate. *Employment, Workplace Relations and Education Committee. Universities in Crisis.* Parliamentary paper No. 217. Canberra: Australian Government Publications Register, 2001.

Pearson, M. "Dollars, Degrees and Dodgy Deals." *Far Eastern Economic Review*, 2004, *167*(43), 20–22.

Poole, M. E., and Langan-Fox, J. *Australian Women and Careers: Psychological and Contextual Influences over the Life Course.* Melbourne: Cambridge University Press, 1997.

Smith, C. "Notes from the Field: Gender Issues in the Management Curriculum—A Survey of Student Experiences." *Gender, Work and Organization*, 2000, *7*(3), 158–167.

Tancred, P. "Literature Review: Formulating Questions." *Management Learning*, 1997, *28*(3), 365–367.

White, K. "Being Ignored: A Case Study of Women in the Professoriate in Australia." Paper presented at the second European Conference on Gender Equality in Higher Education, Zurich, Switzerland, September 2000.

White, K. "Women in the Professoriate in Australia." *International Journal of Organisational Behaviour*, 2001, *3*(2), 64–76.

White, K. "Women and Leadership in Higher Education in Australia." *Tertiary Education and Management*, 2003, *9*(1), 45–60.

APARNA G. HEBBANI *is currently teaching as a lecturer for the University of Queensland, Brisbane, Australia.*

6

This chapter explores identity negotiation by women of color in academe at a predominantly white institution. The author discusses use of the title doctor *as a form of address to manage interactions with graduate students in the college classroom, and the difficulties associated with negotiating and balancing these diverse and complex identities in an oppressive context.*

Black Feminist Thought and Cultural Contracts: Understanding the Intersection and Negotiation of Racial, Gendered, and Professional Identities in the Academy

Tina M. Harris

Colleges and universities are an organizational context in which oppression continues to be perpetuated (Cruz, 2001; Feagin, 1991; Le Roux, 2001). These educational environments are charged with the responsibility of maximizing an individual's intellectual potential and equipping them to be functioning, effective citizens in the real world; however, reality suggests otherwise. Issues of marginalization are ever present and commonplace in higher education even though the efforts to desegregate and integrate are battles of the past. In this context, historically marginalized racial groups are still subjected to varying degrees of prejudice, discrimination, and bias that temporarily divert their personal journey toward intellectual advancement. Students of color and women in higher education deal with barriers designed to impede their progress because of their embodiment of a racialized or gendered identity.

The experiences of students of color (Hine, 1992) in higher education have taken center stage in research addressing issues of marginalization (Gasman and others, 2004). African American (AA) students have been relegated to a racialized existence that forces them to interpret experiences

NEW DIRECTIONS FOR TEACHING AND LEARNING, no. 110, Summer 2007 © Wiley Periodicals, Inc.
Published online in Wiley InterScience (www.interscience.wiley.com) • DOI: 10.1002/tl.274

through a lens of oppression. Similarly, faculty of color also experience marginalization as they traverse the difficult terrain of tenure at a predominately white institution (PWI). They have the daunting task of negotiating among multiple identities (race, gender, professional) while making progress toward tenure (Johnson-Bailey, 1999), an already stressful process. Faculty members of color sometimes operate under the assumption that the motives of others in their academic environment are not always pure, which is evidenced in their interpersonal exchanges. This chapter explores how the racial identities of women of color in academe are negotiated within interpersonal exchanges at a PWI. Attention is given to the use of the title *doctor* as a form of address employed to manage interactions with graduate students in the college classroom. The following sections provide an overview of black feminist thought (BFT) as a conceptual framework. I also discuss how the intersection of race, gender, and professional identities directly affects my experiences as a female faculty member of color. More specifically, I articulate the difficulties associated with negotiating and balancing these diverse and complex identities in an oppressive context. Finally, the concept of cultural contracts is used to contextualize this phenomenon and to offer additional support for the use of BFT in understanding this yet-to-be researched self-reflexive process.

Black Feminist Thought as a Theoretical Lens

Traditional approaches to knowledge in the academy are not the only tool for measuring intellect and knowledge (hooks, 1996). It is through integrating the lived with the researched that this knowledge base can be extended. AA women have achieved visibility by making self-initiated exposure of their ideas and experiences accessible to the masses (Collins, 1996b) by way of fiction books, movies, and print media. hooks (1996) posits that BFT bridges pedagogy and theory for audiences receiving little or no exposure to such critical thought. It is reasonable to assume that this standpoint is essential for including the experiences of a marginalized group in future social science research. Providing intellectual space for their voices to be heard in the community will aid AA women in advancing knowledge about their marginalized experiences in the academy. BFT (Collins, 1993) is the theory I use to contextualize my viewpoints and experiences in academe. Conceptually, gender and existence within a patriarchal system are the commonalities between BFT and feminist theory; however, it is race that divides them. Women from different racial groupings may have similar gendered interpretations of an experience, yet their diverse racial standpoints and pasts create distinctly different experiences, which may offer further evidence of continued marginalization of women of color in a PWI (Collins, 1993). As Collins (1989, 1996a, 1996b) suggests, being a racialized individual (AA) in a predominately white environment calls for the embodiment of a stream of consciousness and awareness of oneself as the proverbial other.

NEW DIRECTIONS FOR TEACHING AND LEARNING • DOI: 10.1002/tl

The salience of one's racial identity, whether internally or externally imposed, forces one to live a "double life," which is the case for an AA woman. She experiences double oppression due to her cultural markers of race and gender. BFT has been espoused and promoted by social scientists as a theory that captures the unique experiences and standpoints of AA women. BFT was born out of the continuing marginalization perpetuated in and by the feminist movement (Spitzack and Carter, 1987), capturing the intersection of race and gender and recognizing the oppressive nature of gender construction and of race as a social construct, which directly affect one's experience. BFT has helped to give voice to a "self-defined collective black women's standpoint about black womanhood" (Collins, 1996a). Thus I propose to give voice to an experience I believe is common to many AA women, and other women of color, at a PWI.

"They Call Me Dr. Tibbs": Engaging the Name Game as Part of Professional Identity

Harlow (2003, p. 357) stated that "black women are confronted with the burden of negotiating femaleness and blackness." These beautiful identities are frequently placed at odds when a person is confronted by competing societal definitions of race and gender, which undoubtedly creates a high level of stress (Smith and Witt, 1993) and makes it difficult for AA female scholars to focus on scholarship while battling the demons of institutional racism. One demon I have battled is the lack of respect a few white students have shown me within and outside of the classroom by not addressing me by my professional title. Since the beginning of my career I have been in the precarious position of defining and defending my professional identity because of my race and gender. Therefore, as I approached graduation for my doctorate I determined it would be in my best interest to be addressed as *Doctor* Harris when occupying space in the academy. I hold strongly to a tradition of respect and reverence that is often lacking in contemporary society. My family, friends, and community formally and informally socialized me to give honor where honor is due. Older persons or authority figures are always addressed as Mister (Mr.), Mrs., Miss (or Ms.), Ma'am, Sir, and Doctor, regardless of context, race, or gender. They are to be respected as those who possesses wisdom and knowledge greater than I do; therefore, they are to be addressed accordingly, and *never* by their first name.

The "Negotiation" Process: Understanding Cultural Contracts

As I reflect on this communication phenomenon that I perceive is a common occurrence among AA and female colleagues who have doctorates, I believe that cultural contracts theory (Jackson, 2002) is the framework that best describes this identity politic. According to Jackson (2004), our multiple

identities are naturally and "constantly being socially constructed and negotiated" (p. 7), and . . . "historically marginalized groups have struggled to
retrieve custody over meanings, especially those meanings pertaining to race.
Agency has never been willingly handed to traditionally underrepresented
groups" (p. 9). Because of our phenotypic features (such as skin color), people of color are mistreated according to the racial hierarchy that maintains
the racial divide in the United States (Kibria, 2000). The dominant group
(that is, whites) thus remains in power, even in our interpersonal interactions. According to the cultural contracts paradigm (Jackson, 2002), our
identities are negotiated and coordinated, and when cultural differences are
present, conflict definitely results, causing relational partners to coordinate
meanings about the relationship "in a fair, equitable manner" (p. 362). Cultural contract negotiation involves a "conscious and mindful process of shifting one's worldview and/or cultural behaviors" (p. 363). "Our bodies signify
racial meaning and our minds comply with social meaning that is culturally
constructed," and because of racialized experiences, marginalized individuals engage in communicative practices "for the sake of preserving, protect-
ing, and defining the self" (p. 363). One makes the decision to conform to
or resist efforts to assimilate to the dominant cultural community (Jackson,
2002), which is partially dependent on "power, boundaries, cultural loyalty,
group identification, maturity" (Jackson, 2004, p. 9).

Cultural contract negotiation involves introspection and, depending on
a variety of contextual cues and variables, choosing between one of three contract typologies: (1) ready-to-sign contract (assimilation), (2) quasi-completed
contract (adaptation), and (3) co-created contract (mutual valuation) (Jackson, 2004, p. 184). "Everyone has 'signed' at least one cultural contract in
his/her life, with every significant encounter, one or more of those cultural
contracts is negotiated" (Jackson, 2004, p. 362). Racialized individuals
are continually placed in contexts where a cultural contract is warranted. The
cultural contract process is an *implicit* agreement of one interactant to ascribe
to the typology that most appropriately addresses how that person chooses to
negotiate his or her racial identity in the company of racially different others.

Deconstructing the Infraction and the Perpetrator

I feel it is imperative to maintain a certain amount of professional distance
between my students and me. The power dynamics of the professor-student
relationship shift when students attempt to define, determine, or shape a
professor's identity through the messages communicated in those interpersonal exchanges. Students activate stereotypes that lower their expectations
of my ability to enact my role as professor (Stangor, Carr, and Kiang, 1998).
To resolve this tension, I have chosen to employ a co-created contract with
my students. To ensure that their stereotypical perceptions of my racial and
gendered identities do not supersede their understandings and perceptions
of my role and identity as their professor, and that my professional identi-

ties are to be respected and valued in our academic cultural community, the use of cultural contracts is essential. As a multilayered other, I feel forced to defend and preserve my integrity and honor when it appears to be devalued or questioned by others. The interpersonal actors in these exchanges vary, yet each one questions my worth as a scholar, academic, human being, and racialized and gendered being.

Cultural contracts are implicit and exist because a racialized individual is forced to assess how his or her identity dictates what communication style, exchanges, and patterns will be activated in interactions with others (Jackson, 2002). I suggest that this theory reveals the significance of using BFT as a framework for interpreting experiences in which we are often marginalized because of our race or gender, among other cultural markers. I would like to explore the cultural contracts theory further by asking the following question: *How does this theory address instances when a person must formally communicate the conditions of a cultural contract with another party?* Although Jackson asserts that cultural contracts are a cognitive process occurring within an individual, it has been my experience that contracts often evolve from an implicit to an explicit articulation of rules guiding interpersonal exchanges where racial differences are framed as problematic because of the behaviors of another (such as a student). As an AA woman, I am often challenged by students to defend my honor as a professional.

Despite my senior status in the relationship, students on occasion deliberately question my intellect, authority, and credibility as their professor. Prompted by natural instincts and prior racialized experiences, I must defend myself and create an argument or stance refuting all efforts to taint my professional identity. Conversations with a few of my white female colleagues on this very topic reveal a distinct disparity in how we interpret our varied experiences; although their professional or gendered identities are lenses through which they gain their understanding, I rarely see or hear of them grappling with the impact that their race has on their professor-student interactions. With the exception of two young white female junior faculty members, very few of my colleagues have expressed a need or desire to employ a cultural contract that clearly delineates their level of engagement with their organizational environment. Although there have been some instances of disrespect, they have been reduced to individual differences or personality clashes. Rather than acknowledge the possibility that these experiences are the result of our otherness, gender and race are perceived as a "last resort" explanation for the insensitive behaviors of others.

I have found the opposite to be true in my experience. When the terms of this unspoken agreement are violated, it is my responsibility to communicate to the violator the "terms" of the contract. Students are informed of their infraction when they assume that a familiarity or interpersonal connection exists that blurs the relational lines of professionalism. Although I am not in the habit of unduly distancing myself from students, this very casual approach to faculty-student interaction breeds

NEW DIRECTIONS FOR TEACHING AND LEARNING • DOI: 10.1002/tl

a culture where familiarity is transformed into a subconscious form of institutional oppression (such as racism) and disrespect that places undue pressure on faculty of color to defend their professional identity.

On several occasions my racial and gendered standpoints have been placed at the forefront of interpersonal interactions with a few graduate and undergraduate students. These interactions have taken place in social and professional contexts and have often been emotionally and psychologically taxing. They have forced me to engage in a stream of consciousness about my race and gender in order to interpret and understand them. In each instance, I was addressed as "Ms." or "Mrs." or "Tina," which communicated to me the speaker's unwillingness to respect me as his or her professor. These students were subconsciously assuming an informal or nonprofessional relationship between us and appeared to conclude that I was unworthy of the respect I was certain would be afforded to a white male colleague. I was prompted to wonder, Am I being treated this way because of my gender? Or is it my race? I engaged in self-talk as I made sense of these recurring interactions that were cast with different actors using the same script. Ultimately I had informal conversations with other female faculty of color and regained a sense of sanity, realizing that my thoughts and feelings were not delusional. As Collins suggests (1996b), this phenomenon is further evidence of another reality occurring frequently in an oppressive society.

Surviving and Celebrating the Matrix

Learning to balance dual identities is often a difficult and stressful process, and if we are to understand the identity negotiation process, racial and gendered standpoints must be recognized and acknowledged. Harlow's in-depth interviews (2003) offer evidence of racial disparities among faculty in their experiences in higher education. Unlike their European American colleagues, AA faculty reported using behaviors or coping strategies that defended them from the uncertainty of potentially racist encounters with students. "By constructing their professional identity selectively, they were able to lessen the individual-level effect of race bias in order to function effectively in the classroom" (Harlow, 2003, p. 361). Although she does not use BFT as her framework, Harlow presents personal testimonies supporting an argument for continued research on the consequences of society-level racial and gender oppression as experienced by AAs in higher education. Harlow gives critical space in her research to the voices of marginalization that too often are ignored by mainstream journals.

Consistent with research on BFT, Harlow (2003) demonstrates how racial and gender oppression forces AA women to develop and use survival strategies in a system designed to help us fail. By utilizing such tactics (for example, overpreparing, citing credentials, and dressing up), professors give power and validation to the "'conventional reality' and 'conventional truth'"

(Harlow, 2003, p. 361) that blacks are inferior. Although some perceive these strategies as compromise, I suggest that they are essential for survival in a racially oppressive environment. It may be inferred that Harlow (2003) is offering examples in which different factors prompt the enactment of cultural contracts, which colleagues and I have done in an attempt to defend and protect ourselves in the academy when our credibility has been questioned. This enactment is an effort to protect ourselves strategically from internal struggles that occur when our multiple identities are placed in direct opposition with one another (Johnson-Bailey, 1999). A potentially negative encounter in which my authority or intellect is, or appears to be, challenged may force me to filter my experience through multiple lenses. I alternate between my racialized, gendered, and professional identities in an attempt to determine which of them most accurately interprets the reality and truth of a particular experience. While I may not be able to determine accurately which identity is in question, I wonder if I am being too sensitive or overly concerned with such issues. Ultimately I resolve to use such strategies because of my trepidations, because these strategies help me manage my dual and coexisting identities.

Discussion

This chapter has discussed two major points that articulate one of many difficulties that AA female faculty experience that make their tenure at PWIs a difficult and isolating experience. I illustrated that BFT is a theoretical framework that articulates how racial and gender identities are at the forefront of that experience (Collins, 1989). I used my personal experience and self-reflection to show how various interpersonal encounters with students have challenged me to interpret those encounters from a racial and gendered standpoint. Our standpoints are an integral part of our individual and collective epistemologies, and they sometimes supersede our professional identities, which makes it incredibly difficult to survive in the academy. Female faculty of color are confronted with experiences in which our racial or gender identities are criticized, making it difficult to nurture our professional identities as scholars and professors. In this case, it is students' (purposeful) failures to acknowledge our professional identities by addressing us by our hard-earned title of *doctor.* These racial encounters can potentially become burdensome and have a cumulative effect on the offended parties (Feagin, 1991, 1992). Instead of dismissing them as infrequent, impersonal infractions, marginalized individuals perceive them as a lifetime of repeated exposure to racial offenses, with an emotional tax that affects their psyche in various ways.

I have also addressed the importance of acknowledging the use of cultural contracts (Jackson, 2002) to cope with behaviors that compromise our professional identities. Although not a tenet of BFT, cultural contracts theory illustrates how racialized and gendered identities cause AA female faculty to use diverse tactics to deal with interpersonal infractions that occur in their organizational environment. Extending the theory, I have suggested the distinct possibility that these contracts experience a transformation from an implicit understanding to an uncomfortable, explicit, and necessary articulation of rules guiding interpersonal exchanges in which racial differences are framed as problematic because of the behaviors of another (such as a student). This may not be the experience of every faculty member of color, yet it is a reality for many. Explicit communication of the boundaries and rules that constitute a cultural contract is often essential for the mental, social, emotional, and professional well-being of the multilayered other.

Conclusion

The politics of race in the academy is a part of the moral fabric of the organizational culture of universities and their departments throughout the nation. A significant body of research on racism offers evidence of this fact. Society continues to be plagued by the social construction of race and a racial hierarchy, both of which influence our perceptions of and interactions with others who are racially different from us. As I have argued, marginalized individuals are frequently subjected to behaviors or interpersonal infractions that further complicate their experience. Although this chapter is limited to a discussion of how faculty preserve their professional identity through the strategic use of cultural contracts, there are other interpersonal phenomena that complicate the workplace experiences and professional success of faculty in higher education. This chapter is not conclusive or generalizable; rather, it sheds light on at least one experience or phenomenon that may contribute to the difficulties associated with recruiting and retaining faculty of color at PWIs. It is only through continued research on and awareness of such institutional barriers that the vicious cycle of modern or subtle racism can be thwarted.

By our very natures, people of color are texts that remain open to interpretation in every aspect of our daily lives. Thus our race functions "as an involuntary sign over which the individual has little or no control, giving off information to others about various aspects of her ethnic identity" (Kibria, 2000, pp. 78–79). The inability to be defined beyond a racial identity is problematic when the self or others restrict one's nature to a single identity (Vandenbroeck, 2000). Placing such limitations on individuals who are attempting to understand their multiple identities creates racial boundaries that are impermeable and difficult to overcome (Johnson-Bailey, 1999). The invisible glass ceiling is not the only barrier that impedes the professional success of faculty of color. It is the discourteous and subtle innuendos of inferiority conveyed through public and private discourses that make negative experiences in higher education very difficult to overcome.

Much like this volume, devoting intellectual space to understanding the complexities of identity negotiation for academics of color is critical to the efforts of colleges and universities to diversify their faculties and student bodies. Members of these marginalized communities are morally obligated to use our epistemological tools (such as BFT) (Collins, 1989) to engage in public discourse about this underresearched phenomenon. Such discourse will act as a springboard for identifying problems that plague faculty of color and for offering solutions that create intellectual spaces that affirm and support our multiple and complex identities. Our coping strategies and mechanisms are diverse, and no one approach will resolve the dilemma of identity negotiation within the academy. There are certainly some instances in which we are disrespected. These are frequently reduced to matters of individual differences or personality clashes. Instead of considering that disrespectful behaviors may be due to a person's otherness, they are viewed as being a natural part of the world of academe and not a manifestation of blatant forms of racial or gender oppression.

The pain and frustration that come with these varied encounters remain a constant barrier or hurdle to our survival in the ivory jungle. It is my hope that this chapter will challenge administrators and faculty alike at PWIs to engage in critical discourse, dialogue, and self-reflection about their roles in perpetuating the cycle of oppression. Such strategies may contribute to our understanding of the difficulties associated with recruiting and retaining faculty and students of color, and lead to at least one safe space where we can identify how individuals cope with and manage the stressors of being the "other" in the ivory tower.

References

Collins, P. H. "The Social Construction of Black Feminist Thought." *Signs: Journal of Women in Culture and Society,* 1989, *14*(4), 745–773.

Collins, P. H. *Black Feminist Thought: Knowledge, Consciousness, and the Politics of Empowerment.* New York: Routledge, 1993.

Collins, P. H. "Sociological Visions and Revisions." *Contemporary Sociology,* 1996a, *25*(3), 328–331.

Collins, P. H. "What's in a Name? Womanism, Black Feminism, and Beyond." *Black Scholar,* 1996b, *26*(1), 9–17.

Cruz, C. "Toward an Epistemology of a Brown Body." *Qualitative Studies in Education,* 2001, *14*(5), 357–669.

Feagin, J. R. "The Continuing Significance of Race: Antiblack Discrimination in Public Places." *American Sociological Review,* 1991, *56*(1), 101–116.

Feagin, J. R. "The Continuing Significance of Racism: Discrimination Against Black Students in White Colleges." *Journal of Black Studies,* 1992, *22*(4), 546–578.

Gasman, M., Gerstl-Pepin, C., Anderson-Thompkins, S., Rasheed, L., and Hathaway, K. "Negotiating Power, Developing Trust: Transgressing Race and Status in the Academy." *Teachers College Record,* 2004, *106*(4), 689–715.

Harlow, R. "Race Doesn't Matter, but. . . .": The Effect of Race on Professors' Experiences and Emotion Management in the Undergraduate College Classroom." *Social Psychology Quarterly,* 2003, *66*(4), 348–363.

Hine, D. C. "The Black Studies Movement: Afrocentric-Traditionalist-Feminist Paradigms for the Next Stage." *Black Scholar,* 1992, *22*(3), 11–18.

hooks, b. "Sisterhood: Beyond Public and Private." *Signs: Women in Culture and Society,* 1996, *21*(4), 814–829.

Jackson, R. L. "Cultural Contracts Theory: Toward an Understanding of Identity Negotiation." *Communication Quarterly,* 2002, *50*(3/4), 359–367.

Jackson, R. L. "Negotiating and Mediating Constructions of Racial Identities." *Review of Communication,* 2004, *4*(1/2), 6–15.

Johnson-Bailey, J. "The Ties That Bind and the Shackles That Separate: Race, Gender, Class, and Color in a Research Process." *International Journal of Qualitative Studies in Education,* 1999, *12*(6), 660–671.

Kibria, N. "Race, Ethnic Options, and Ethnic Binds: Identity Negotiations of Second-Generation Chinese and Korean Americans." *Sociological Perspectives,* 2000, *43*(1), 77–95.

Le Roux, J. "Social Dynamics of the Multicultural Classroom." *Intercultural Education,* 2001, *12*(3), 273–288.

Smith, E., and Witt, S. "A Comparative Study of Occupational Stress Among African American and White University Faculty: A Research Note. *Research in Higher Education,* 1993, *34,* 229–241.

Spitzack, C., and Carter, K. "Women in Communication Studies: A Typology for Revision." *Quarterly Journal of Speech,* 1987, *73*(4), 401–423.

Stangor, C., Carr, C., and Kiang, L. "Activating Stereotypes Undermines Task Performance Expectations." *Journal of Personality and Social Psychology,* 1998, *75*(5), 1191–1197.

Vandenbroeck, M. "Self-Awareness, Cultural Identity and Connectedness: Three Terms to (Re)define in Anti-Bias Work." Paper presented at the tenth European Conference on Quality in Early Childhood Education (European Early Childhood Education Research Association) Conference, London, Aug. 29–Sept. 1, 2000.

TINA M. HARRIS *is associate professor of communication at the University of Georgia, with research expertise in interracial and intercultural communication, race and pedagogy, and religious frameworks in health communication.*

NEW DIRECTIONS FOR TEACHING AND LEARNING • DOI: 10.1002/tl

7

Internationalization of college classrooms challenges international instructors, students, and their relationships. This chapter addresses these challenges and offers strategies for overcoming them.

Being an Interculturally Competent Instructor in the United States: Issues of Classroom Dynamics and Appropriateness, and Recommendations for International Instructors

Claudia Ladeira McCalman

During the last two decades an increasing number of international faculty specializing in different disciplines have been hired by U.S. institutions of higher education. Most of these instructors have been college educated in their native countries but have come to the United States for graduate studies and then earned doctoral degrees from U.S. institutions. Although some of them return to their places of origin, many remain in this country and follow academic careers at teaching or research universities (Bresnahan and Kim, 1993; MacLennan, 2002). At the macrolevel, the absorption of this specialized workforce contributes to globalization in education. At the microlevel, it enhances the internationalization of college classrooms in the United States and brings other practical implications. This chapter focuses on the microlevel, the internationalization of college classrooms in the United States—already a common phenomenon in Europe and Australia.

Several questions come to mind when one ponders the internationalization process and the intercultural relations embedded in it. On the one hand, are U.S. students aware of the need to become prepared to interact and work in an international community? It appears that our students are

not aware of the need for competence in intercultural communication or to acquire an education that will equip them to become effective leaders in the global community. McGray (2006) asserts that the culprit of this intercultural incompetence is the provincialism of our school system and curriculum. Further, he mentions President George W. Bush's 2006 concerns and efforts to review previous government reports such as *Strength Through Wisdom* (President's Commission on Foreign Language and International Studies, 1979) with the possibility of reconsidering implementation of foreign language programs and international experiences as crucial to students' education, beginning in elementary school. On the other hand, are international instructors interpersonally and pedagogically equipped to work with our college students? What challenges do they face when interacting with their students? What do they need to know in terms of strategies to foster a classroom climate that is conducive to learning? Throughout the chapter I discuss intercultural and interpersonal challenges emerging from the internationalization of our classroom process, and I suggest ways in which instructors can productively deal with those challenges.

Challenges to Globalization and the International Faculty Experience

Bringing globalization to the American classroom challenges the educational system, international instructors, and students. This process will take time and requires curriculum change beginning in elementary or middle school. Without global awareness, a myopic view of the world and discomfort with the unknown will prevail. This section addresses three themes: (1) students' naïveté and lack of interest, (2) their difficulty in accepting nonnative instructors, and (3) students' perceptions of instructors' effectiveness.

Naïveté and Lack of Interest. Naïveté and lack of interest are prompted by a curriculum that minimizes world issues, thus becoming a stumbling block to awareness of world citizenship (McGray, 2006; Otten, 2003). An example of this outcome occurred in 2001 in one of my graduate classes at a Midwestern university. I remember vividly the students' apathy concerning any need to be aware that not all people around the globe are American sympathizers. To my surprise, a female graduate student expressed in class her belief that "Americans are generally loved and respected abroad"—a belief apparently held by most of the students. That attitude changed abruptly, however, when five months later we all saw in the media the horrifying images of the 9/11 terrorist attacks in New York and Washington, D.C.

Receptivity and Acceptance. Bringing international issues and people to our classrooms is even more challenging when we face students' resistance to and lack of curiosity about issues unfamiliar to them. One example is the level of receptivity to and acceptance of nonnative instructors, many of whom are teaching English as a second language. Rubin and Smith (1990) found that teachers' ethnicity and choice of topic were more important determinants of undergraduates' attitudes than accentedness. It appears that many of the negative behaviors of undergraduates toward international teaching assistants (ITAs) tend to continue when these international students stay in the United States and follow academic careers.

What are the predictors of receptivity and resistance to ITAs and other international faculty members? Bresnahan and Kim (1993) assert that the accentedness variable by itself fails to explain why some students are receptive to international instructors and others are not. They found that two personality traits, authoritarianism and dogmatism, were strong predictors of low receptivity to internationals. Authoritarians embrace uncritical acceptance of the status quo and see outside interference as a threat to maintenance of lifestyle. Dogmatic personalities have low tolerance for ambiguity and feel uncomfortable with internationals.

Moreover, Caucasian students rated Asian American instructors less credible and less intelligible than European American instructors (Rubin, 1998). In another study, African American teachers were challenged more often than European American teachers concerning teaching credentials and classroom authority (Hendrix, 1998). Acceptance takes time, effort, tenacity, and experience on the part of the instructor. Hope and *self-efficacy* (the inner belief that one has the skills to succeed) are necessary ingredients for nonnative instructors to succeed (see Bandura, 1989).

Perceived Teacher Effectiveness. Comparing domestic and international college instructors on several other categories of perceived teacher effectiveness, such as affect toward the teacher, affect toward the content of the class, and others, McCroskey (2002, p. 74) found that domestic teachers were perceived as more effective than international instructors, and that "students clearly have less positive affect for courses taught by international teachers, and less positive affect toward those teachers." Rubin and Smith (1990) also found that, although not as important as teachers' ethnicity and topic choice, the level of perceived English accentedness had an impact on how students rated the teaching competency of international instructors.

It appears that complex factors contribute to students' perceptions of disciplines taught by an accented speaker. Yook and Albert (1999), studying international instructors and the interrelatedness of intercultural training, cognition, and emotion, found a relationship between emotions and students' ratings of international teachers' competence. Emotions affected evaluations of teachers' competence and students' comprehension. Happiness prompted higher evaluations and greater comprehension of content.

Sadness prompted both lower evaluations and poorer content comprehension. Thus it may be possible that the dissimilarity between students and instructors regarding ethnicity, country of origin, levels of cross-cultural exposure, and first language can prompt negative emotions such as "anxiety and uncertainty" (Gudykunst, 1988). Such uncomfortable feelings may develop into "intercultural communication apprehension" (Neuliep and McCroskey, 1997). Consequently, this apprehension may influence students' evaluation of instruction by biasing their perceptions of teachers' effectiveness and affecting the scoring of international instructors (McCroskey, 2002) and possibly of other instructors of color. However, two questions remain unanswered by McCroskey's study: "Are the differences in perceived teacher effectiveness a function of real differences in the communication behaviors of teachers? Are they a function of various biases of the students?" (p. 65). Research is still needed on these subtopics. The next section explains potential variables affecting undergraduates' satisfaction with, receptivity to, and tolerance of their "different" instructors.

Satisfaction, Receptivity, and Tolerance

What accounts for the low levels of satisfaction with, receptivity to, and tolerance of the international instructor? As mentioned in the last section, negative perceptions may be prompted by the discomfort that Gudykunst (1988) and Neuliep and McCroskey (1997) named *intercultural communication apprehension*. Specifically, this term refers to the anxiety and uncertainty arousal that are typical of intercultural communication contexts. Having an international instructor in charge of the classroom requires a stretch of students' comfort zones, that is, their biases and stereotypes, which are capable of destroying any potential effectiveness of such interactions. Moreover, some undergraduates assume that ITAs and international professors come from less developed societies to learn in the United States because of our superior educational system (Brislin, 1990; McCroskey, 2002). As Mestenhauser (1983) further explains, the bottom line is that these internationals are in the United States to learn from us and not to teach us. Psychologically this places international instructors in a submissive position, reinforcing students' beliefs in the lack of equity among the parties (Brislin, 1990).

Perceived Competence. What can instructors teaching in a second language do to be perceived as more effective in the classroom? The first step is to train the teacher; the second is to train the student. Although intercultural orientation programs exist at larger universities, little attention is paid at the level of the institution to teaching preparation for international professors. Regarding training for undergraduates, Yook and Albert (1999) have suggested that intercultural sensitivity training could help. Participating in study-abroad programs is also beneficial (Pennington and Wildermuth, 2005). Such training would contribute to reducing U.S. undergraduates' ethnocentrism, which in McCroskey's study (2002) was the strongest variable in predicting students' negative perceptions of international instructors.

Although intercultural communication theory and previous empirical research help to explain why domestic college teachers are perceived as more effective than international teachers, the reasons for such perceived differences are not clear. McCroskey (2002) concluded that besides ethnocentrism, perhaps certain instructional communication behaviors could be responsible for the less positive perceptions of effectiveness of international instructors.

NEW DIRECTIONS FOR TEACHING AND LEARNING • DOI: 10.1002/tl

Specific teaching behaviors of international instructors that may be different from those of native teachers and need adaptation to fit U.S. classrooms are generally addressed in ITA training. Such teaching behaviors include organization and clarity of presentation, use of practical examples, use of contexts familiar to students, teachers' presence (confidence, appropriate authority, rapport with audience), teachers' methods of handling questions, and clarity of response to questions (Smith, Meyers, and Burkhalter, 1992). Female instructors may more often deal with other relational issues, such as power and incivility, which are addressed in the next section.

Gender and Power in the Classroom. In the field of human communication a large number of international faculty are females. One of the issues that concerns us as female faculty is the issue of power and incivility, which are experienced in various degrees by almost all faculty members (Alexander-Snow, 2004). Such behavior can be detrimental to teachers' performance, students' learning, and course evaluations. Investigations into causes of incivility (Boise, 1996) suggest that it may be prompted by a teacher's lack of immediacy. Because Boise was not investigating international female instructors or female faculty of color, I believe that Alexander-Snow's suggestion of adding a cultural dimension to Boise's work is plausible. Alexander Snow asserts that cultural perceptions play an important role in understanding this type of behavior in the classroom. We also need to consider Aries's clarification (1996) that stereotypical beliefs about minority people can lead to expectations about how people should conduct themselves that are based on their cultural identities. I therefore agree with Alexander-Snow (2004) when she poses that believing that just by showing immediacy in the classroom the "different instructor" is going to prompt civility is a very simplistic approach in an intercultural classroom.

Incivility reflects power struggles between students and teachers. If the teacher's behavior or profile is a mismatch to what students expect, it may propitiate incivility, no matter how much prosocial behavior the female faculty member uses with her students. Thus, unlike their white male colleagues, international female faculty must be aware of how their cultural identities and gender complicate the classroom environment. They know that there is a high probability that their credibility and authority will be questioned. Alexander-Snow (2004) addresses this point, adding that students uncomfortable with having the material taught by a member of a subordinate group will be more likely to practice incivility. In the next sections I present the construct of communication competence and a feminist pedagogy that I practice in my classrooms to narrow the gap between my students and me.

Strategies: Narrowing the Gap

Effective communication in intercultural classrooms requires knowledge of the cultures involved. Especially challenging for international female faculty are cross-cultural situations in which only one party involved understands the cultural schema and expectations of the others. Because U.S. students generally lack knowledge and curiosity about the culture of the "different" instructor, the role of narrowing the cultural gap is the sole effort and responsibility of the instructor. In the next section I suggest a feminist perspective on teaching that I have adopted in my work, and I call on international women of color in academia to establish a self-support system to overcome challenges they may encounter.

Intercultural Competence in the Classroom. Effective teaching begins with the teacher. My experience has been that in order to know better the cultural traits of my U.S. students, I first needed to know the traits of my own (original) culture. Only then can I reflect on our differences and adapt to their background and needs. It has also been my experience that students in various geographic areas in the United States require specific adaptations. The reason is that cultural dimensions such as individualism or collectivism, time orientation, and other dimensions will differ by degrees in different geographic areas of the country. These dimensions require constant adaptation depending on the state and region.

In the intercultural classroom, communication competence is the process by which the instructor continually strives to achieve the ability to work effectively and appropriately within the cultural context of his or her students. For instance, Campinha-Bacote's approach (2001) to intercultural competence demands that we see ourselves as in the process of becoming culturally competent rather than believing we are already competent. A route to competence includes *awareness* of our own culture, and of how wide the cultural gap is between others and us. Another variable is our *knowledge* about the culture and worldview of the other. My choice of appropriate communication is the skill of making use of certain strategies in a sensitive, nonjudgmental manner. Useful also is the *motivation* to learn about U.S. culture and my students, to ask them to express their worldviews, opinions, and expectations in classroom discussions. Conversely, intercultural competence involves prompting in U.S. students an interest in "different" people, and encouraging them to adopt the idea of becoming a global citizen. This approach includes giving examples of how people in other areas of the world might have different ways of solving the same problem.

Feminist Pedagogy. I adopt in my work a feminist perspective on teaching and learning. Feminism analyzes and opposes diverse forms of oppression. In this context, feminism, as Wood (1989) embraces it, includes the assumption that diversity is valuable and that multiple ways of knowing are acceptable because they reflect our standpoint in life. I also make clear for them that in my classes (for example, Gender Communication, and Diversity and Organizational Culture) all students' voices are heard and that an interactive style of teaching is employed. I teach that we need to learn about life from the perspective and experiences of others because our perspective and experiences alone give us a myopic, incomplete view of reality. I try to make my students see that we need to move from a gender-based *machista,* patriarchal view of oppression to a perspective that respects diverse worldviews.

My use of feminist pedagogy in the classroom enforces an integrative, collaborative, respectful, nonauthoritarian process of teaching and learning, as Kenway and Modra's (1992) work suggests. In order to create such safe space, I value and recognize the unique life perspective and contribution of each individual in the class and let students know that they should be active participants in the learning process. Two main strategies have helped me in dealing with social power struggles in the classroom when they have sporadically happened, mainly in the undergraduate freshman classes. The first strategy is the *community* approach, and the second is the *diplomat* approach.

The community strategy is generally employed when I spot resistance from one person or a small group of freshmen (a clique of two or three). Now and then I encounter disruptive students to whom the teacher or her message or her accent may be too funny or decoded with sarcasm. As far as I can remember, the most disruptive students in my career have been young white males, also at the freshman or sophomore levels. Once I observe their behavior, I act immediately and try to keep those students engaged and busy. I do not confront them but instead ask (in front of the class) for their collaboration as participants in our community. Their nonverbal behavior after the invitation shows surprise. They reluctantly accept the invitation. I make sure that I add several inclusive pronouns, such as "we," "our class," "us," and "our objectives," when I talk to the class. The task in which they will be collaborators is to be time manager for the public speakers that semester or that week. They serve their function in the beginning somewhat reluctantly. However, after about three classes they begin volunteering for the task. I tell the class that during that stipulated time of day they will be "in charge" of when speakers should start their presentation, because "I am too busy" grading and going through the speech evaluation form for every speaker. They take the task seriously and do a good job. By delegating power for a small amount of time and for a specific task, I enable my formerly disruptive students to feel empowered and engaged, and to become responsible students for the rest of the semester. If the disruption comes from a small group, I ask them to take turns being the time manager for the speakers that week or semester. I also highlight that this work is voluntary.

The diplomat strategy works best for students who have never been exposed to an international person or environment. These students may behave very critically or judgmentally. This is a good strategy for the parochial students, who are always giggling in the corner of the room with friends. For them everything is funny when they have an international professor who speaks in accented English. For this type of people in the audience I begin with comparisons, suggesting that they could one day be working for a multinational corporation, or even the United Nations. I begin by saying that "our way of solving problems is just one way," but people around the world solve problems in different ways using the different types and amounts of resources available to them. Sometimes we do not solve problems because we may not have the resources. Then I explain the role of culture in giving us scripts for meaning and behavior. Next I ask for contributions from people who have lived in other states of this country, then from those who have lived in other countries or who have participated in a study-abroad program. We then compare and contrast how we do "this" in Latin America. The students give me the corresponding response for the United States, such as how we pronounce a particular word or what the word is in Portuguese or Spanish, and what the corresponding word or pronunciation is in English. This strategy engages them in the discipline, and they demonstrate satisfaction in learning something that is "different."

Support Groups for International Women and Women of Color. This last section is a call to other international women and women of color in academia to found a base of self-help groups for support and mentoring. In these support coalitions, female faculty who are more experienced would provide information and mentorship. Their members could suggest and engage in diverse ways of combating forms of oppression and inequality in academia, and learn strategies for coping with challenging situations and strategies for job effectiveness.

These types of coalitions with other diverse women can compensate for barriers such as information deficiency. Many international and women of color feel uninformed because of limited access to or exclusion from informal networks. Limited access to the "grapevine" has many disadvantages, including restricted knowledge of issues at the departmental, college, and university levels, such as the experiences of other faculty members with classroom management challenges and how they have solved them; issues of academic publishing, tenure, and promotion; and mobility within the university. Another barrier for international women and women of color is the difficulty of finding a female mentoring relationship that can be beneficial academically and psychosocially, and ultimately empowering. This nonformal education received from mentors can be used for positive, transformative purposes.

Conclusion

What do international female instructors need to know to be interpersonally and pedagogically equipped to do an effective job? We need to develop teaching skills that are compatible with those of the host culture, effective verbal and nonverbal communication skills, and sensitivity to intercultural differences. Throughout this chapter I have highlighted the importance of flexibility, perceptiveness, control, awareness, adaptability, and the instructor's need to gain intercultural communication competence in the classroom. This competence does not come easily. It takes time, perseverance, and experience. Two other important strategies are to adopt a feminist pedagogy in the classroom and to search for coalition with and the support of other international feminists and feminists of color who understand our reality, including our contributions and challenges, with whom we can brainstorm for solutions.

References

Alexander-Snow, M. "Dynamics of Gender, Ethnicity, and Race in Understanding Classroom Incivility." In J. M. Braxton and A. E. Bayer (eds.), *Addressing Faculty and Student Classroom Improprieties*. New Directions for Teaching and Learning, no. 99. San Francisco: Jossey-Bass, 2004.

Aries, E. *Men and Women in Interaction: Reconsidering the Differences*. New York: Oxford University Press, 1996.

Bandura, A. "Self-Regulation of Motivation and Action Through Internal Standards and Goal Systems." In L. A. Pervin (ed.), *Goal Concepts in Personality and Social Psychology*. Hillsdale, N.J.: Erlbaum, 1989.

Boise, R. "Classroom Incivilities." *Research in Higher Education*, 1996, *37*(4), 453–485.

Bresnahan, M. I., and Kim, M. S. "Predictors of Receptivity and Resistance Toward International Teaching Assistants." *Journal of Asian Pacific Communication*, 1993, *4*(1), 3–14.

Brislin, R. W. *Applied Cross-Cultural Psychology*. Newbury Park, Calif.: Sage, 1990.

Campinha-Bacote, J. "The Process of Cultural Competence in the Delivery of Healthcare: A Model of Care. *Journal of Transcultural Nursing*, 2001, *13*, 181–184.

Gudykunst, W. B. "Uncertainty and Anxiety." In Y. Y. Kim and W. B. Gudykunst (eds.), *Theories in Intercultural Communication*. Newbury Park, Calif.: Sage, 1988.

Hendrix, K. G. "Student Perceptions of the Influence of Race on Professor Credibility." *Journal of Black Studies*, 1998, *28*, 738–764.

Kenway, J., & Modra, H. "Feminist Pedagogy and Emancipatory Possibilities." In C. Luke and J. Gore (eds.), *Feminisms and Critical Pedagogy*. New York: Routledge, 1992.

MacLennan, J. "There's a Lizard in My Living Room and a Pigeon in My Classroom: A Personal Reflection on What It Takes to Teach in a Different Culture." *Journal of Intercultural Communication Research*, 2002, *31*(2), 13–28.

McCroskey, L. L. "Domestic and International College Instructors: An Examination of Perceived Differences and Their Correlates." *Journal of Intercultural Communication Research*, 2002, *31*(2), 63–83.

McGray, D. "Lost in America." *Foreign Policy*, 2006, *154*, 40–48.

Mestenhauser, J. A. "Learning from Sojourners." In D. Landis and R. W. Brislin (eds.), *Handbook of Intercultural Training*, Vol. 2. New York: Pergamon, 1983.

Neuliep, J. W., and McCroskey, J. C. "The Development of Intercultural and Interethnic Communication Apprehension Scales." *Communication Research Reports*, 1997, *14*, 145–156.

Otten, M. "Intercultural Learning and Diversity in Higher Education." *Journal of Studies in International Education*, 2003, *7*(1), 12–26.

Pennington, B., and Wildermuth, S. "Three Weeks There and Back Again: A Qualitative Investigation of the Impact of Short-Term Travel/Study on the Development of Intercultural Communication Competency." *Journal of Intercultural Communication Research*, 2005, *34*(3), 166–183.

President's Commission on Foreign Language and International Studies. *Strength Through Wisdom: A Critique of U.S. Capability*. Washington, D.C.: U.S. Government Printing Office, 1979.

Rubin, D. L. "Help! My Professor (or Doctor or Boss) Doesn't Talk English!" In J. M. Nakayama and L. Flores (eds.), *Readings in Cultural Contexts*. Mountain View, Calif.: Mayfield, 1998.

Rubin, D. L., and Smith, K. A. "Effects of Accent, Ethnicity, and Lecture Topic on Undergraduates' Perceptions of Non-Native English Speaking Teaching Assistants." *International Journal of Intercultural Relations*, 1990, *14*, 337–353.

Smith, J., Meyers, C., and Burkhalter, A. J. *Communicate: Strategies for International Teaching Assistants.* Englewood Cliffs, N.J.: Regents/Prentice Hall, 1992.

Wood, J. "Feminist Pedagogy in Interpersonal Communication Courses." Paper presented at the Speech Communication Association Conference, San Francisco, November 1989.

Yook, E. L., and Albert, R. D. "Perceptions of International Teaching Assistants: The Interrelatedness of Intercultural Training, Cognition, and Emotion." *Communication Education,* 1999, *48,* 1–17.

CLAUDIA LADEIRA MCCALMAN earned her doctorate in speech communication from Pennsylvania State University, teaches communication at Southeastern Louisiana University, and conducts research about the role of culture in several contexts, including health communication.

*Being a Hispanic female faculty member in South Texas
can be a challenge. This chapter discusses three pedagogical tools (caring, challenging, and consulting) that we use
to create a classroom climate that enhances Hispanic students' success by engaging and motivating them to succeed in one of the poorest areas of the country.*

Women of Color Teaching Students of Color: Creating an Effective Classroom Climate Through Caring, Challenging, and Consulting

Dora E. Saavedra, Marisa L. Saavedra

The population of the Rio Grande Valley of South Texas, according to the U.S. Census of Population and Housing (U.S. Bureau of the Census, 2002), is approximately 88 percent Hispanic. It is also an area in which approximately 35.7 percent of the population lives below the poverty line. The University of Texas-Pan American and South Texas College are two institutions of higher education that serve this population. Hispanics constitute more than 85 percent of the enrollment at both institutions, and many of the students at both institutions are the first generation in their families to go to college from economically disadvantaged backgrounds. In addition, many of these students come from Spanish-speaking households. It is this cultural context that presents challenges and rewards to the faculty who serve these students. This chapter focuses briefly on identifying some of the challenges of being Hispanic female faculty members in this cultural context, and on how we handle these challenges. We then discuss three major pedagogical tools (caring, challenging, and consulting) that we use to create a classroom climate that enhances student success by engaging and motivating them to succeed in one of the poorest areas of the country. Each of these pedagogical tools is broken down into its individual components and discussed, along with research material and examples to support them.

NEW DIRECTIONS FOR TEACHING AND LEARNING, no. 110, Summer 2007 © Wiley Periodicals, Inc.
Published online in Wiley InterScience (www.interscience.wiley.com) • DOI: 10.1002/tl.276

The Challenges of Teaching in a Hispanic Culture

Institutions of higher learning often create an environment in which students (as well as faculty) of color encounter numerous challenges and difficulties. Their status as "others" in society often serves to marginalize them as learners within the educational environment. The students in our classrooms are mostly first-generation college students who for the most part come from the Rio Grande Valley or northern Mexico. As a general rule, many of these students are also classified as economically disadvantaged. For many of them English is a second language. In addition, the male Hispanic students may come from traditional homes where negative *machismo* attitudes are deeply ingrained, which may interfere with their acceptance of a female instructor. These challenges, however, can be turned into opportunities for effective classroom management. The Hispanic culture is, in general, known to be respectful of authority and relationship oriented. Instructors are therefore in a position to help students navigate through their academic careers and overcome their challenges. For instance, an instructor's sensitivity to first-generation issues may mean that she or he needs to provide students with structure and clarity in the classroom to offset their lack of experience in the higher education context. Also, in our situation, the issue of English being a second language can be turned into a positive one by occasionally relating to the students in Spanish—taking care, of course, that the non-Spanish speakers in the classroom are not excluded. Finally, instructors need to remember that *macho* attitudes exist in all cultures, not just in the Hispanic culture. In fact, it is important to remember that these positive and negative stereotypes are of course just that—stereotypes—and that part of the educational process is to work beyond assumptions based on stereotypes.

In addition to the challenges we face as faculty, there are also advantages to working in a Hispanic-serving institution and being Hispanic women. First, we share an ethnic heritage with our students; thus, students perceive us as being similar to them in language and cultural background (McCroskey, 1998). Our common ethnic heritage helps us build a relationship with our students. In addition, we share with them a bilingual and bicultural orientation. The Texas-Mexico border is porous, with many Mexicans and Mexican Americans traveling back and forth between the two countries with little regard for the political border that exists, because they have family and roots on both sides of the border. Finally, our family generational histories are similar to those of our students. These histories include relatives who were immigrants to this country, relatives who have been migrant farmworkers, and relatives who have struggled to become the first in their family to attain a higher education. These are the common-ground elements that help us relate to our students and their backgrounds.

Now that we have looked at some of the challenges and advantages of being Hispanic female instructors, let us turn to a general overview of what

NEW DIRECTIONS FOR TEACHING AND LEARNING • DOI: 10.1002/tl

the literature tells us is effective teaching. We will then cover the three pedagogical tools we mentioned earlier—caring, challenging, and consulting.

What Are Effective Teaching Behaviors That Create a Caring Classroom Climate?

One of the most important elements of an effective classroom environment is an atmosphere in which students feel valued and respected. This section addresses the instructor behaviors that contribute to creating a caring classroom climate.

Nussbaum (1992, p. 167) describes effective teacher behaviors as "those in-class behaviors of the teacher that are related directly either to positive student outcomes or [to] positive evaluations of teaching." More specifically, these behaviors are generally described as including teacher immediacy, teacher clarity, teacher's use of humor, teacher communicator style, and teacher use of narratives (Andersen, 1979; Nussbaum, 1984; Nussbaum, Comadena, and Holladay, 1987). All of these behaviors are supported by various researchers as behaviors that enhance teaching effectiveness in the classroom. These are all behaviors that we strive to use in our classrooms.

In general, teacher immediacy is important when working with any population, yet it becomes increasingly important when working with Hispanic students who are the first in their families to attend college. It is particularly important to know each student's name and to be able to express how much we care about them as human beings. Eye contact, smiles, and other positive nonverbals are essential in creating a safe communication climate for these students. Verbally we affirm their participation, and we get to know their stories, their opinions, and their challenges. Our classroom evaluations give voice to our success in these areas. As one student wrote, "Towards the end of each class session, you make the class feel welcome to discuss any further issues. Students who have that bond or level of comfort in the classroom are able to drop that guard that many tend to have. This way, students can broaden their minds at a much more effective level. Allowing the class to be open and flexible is effective in a caring way."

Teacher clarity is also essential in that students need explicit instruction and well-structured assignments in order to succeed (Sidelinger and McCroskey, 1997). This means that assignments should be given to them both orally and in writing. Because these students tend to be global learners, exemplars are useful in the form of videos or handouts. In fact, it is important to note that exemplars are useful to all students, but in particular to students whose educational experiences have been limited.

Humor in the classroom is also important to creating a positive classroom climate. Students often enjoy the novelty and the break in routine when the instructor tells a story or joke to enhance course content. This approach has been shown to heighten students' interest, thus leading to enhanced memory of the material (Kintsch and Bates, 1977). Both of us are comfortable not only talking about funny incidents but also making fun of ourselves. Sharing humorous stories helps us as instructors to connect with our students.

Teacher communication style has also been examined by many scholars to determine its effect on teacher effectiveness (Powers, Nitcavic, and Koerner, 1990). The dramatic and relaxed communication style has garnered particular attention. In a 1980 study, Norton and Nussbaum found that certain dramatic behaviors—such as the ability to control the mood of the class, to tell a good story, and to get students to laugh—are systematically associated with effective teachers. Later, Nussbaum (1982) found that the most effective teachers utilize a dramatic and relaxed communication. These teachers use jokes, stories, and verbal exaggeration to create an open and comfortable (as opposed to tense) learning environment for their students. Nussbaum, Comadena, and Holladay (1987) found that effective teachers who employ a dramatic teaching style use more energy, humor, self-disclosure, and narrative activity while teaching. We employ dramatic behaviors within a relaxed and supportive classroom setting to help us motivate students and encourage their participation.

Perry, Abrami, and Levanthal's study (1979) revealed that teacher expressiveness, a major element of the dramatic teaching style, affected student ratings of the professor and student achievement in the class. If a student rates a professor highly, chances are the student has an affinity for the professor and will work hard to satisfy the teacher's requirements. Norton (1983) also found that students pay more attention to a teacher who utilizes a dramatic style because they are given the impression that something significant and remarkable is happening in the classroom, which in turn creates the ideal teaching and learning environment—one in which students participate, are involved, and are excited about the material they are learning. The second author's students frequently comment that she makes learning fun.

Another study (Javidi, Downs, and Nussbaum, 1988) that examined teachers' use of dramatic behaviors noted the importance of narrative in the classroom. The results of the study revealed that award-winning college teachers included 5.26 narratives within fifty minutes of lecturing, and most of these narratives were used to clarify the class material. Overall, results suggest that teacher use of narrative, as well as other dramatic behaviors, is a key factor of teaching effectiveness. Teachers' use of narrative in the classroom does not simply have benefits in terms of learning and comprehension. Affective learning or an improved attitude toward the professor and the class material is another possible outcome of implementing narrative in lectures (Krathwohl, Bloom, and Masia, 1964). Meier and Feldhusen (1979) also suggested that highly expressive teachers are better liked by students, and that short-term achievement is more likely to increase when a student is in contact with a highly expressive instructor. We have both been described by our students as hilarious, expressive, and great storytellers.

It is clear then that the dramatic behaviors of highly expressive teachers, such as using storytelling or narratives in the classroom, can help promote student engagement and, in turn, motivation. This is especially important in the classroom wherein the vast majority of students' families do not have a history of postsecondary education. Using intergenerational narratives of our own families has been very helpful. For example, the first author's mother became a widow at age forty, and at age forty-two, with six children ranging in age from nine to twenty-one, started college and went on to become a bilingual first-grade teacher for twenty years before retiring. Many of the nontraditional-aged students and the single mothers in the classroom relate to this story. For Hispanics, *la familia* is of primary importance, and attending college can promote guilt for not spending more time with family. Sharing with students the success stories of others who have struggled and succeeded helps them to know that their struggles can have a happy ending.

Students' course comments about our teaching have included the following:

Her care is evident in the respect she allows each of us when we speak.
She always notices when a student is missing. That makes students care to go to class more often.
She realizes that everyone learns differently, and she is willing to adapt to it.
She understands life issues.
She makes herself available and approachable when students need to talk to her and present their problems.

What Are Effective Teaching Behaviors That Create a Challenging Classroom Climate?

In this section we discuss the importance of setting high expectations, helping students to reframe their educational experiences cognitively in order to engage and motivate them to succeed, and establishing credibility in the classroom. Here we share how we set the stage for the learning of difficult and complex theoretical material.

As facilitators of learning in the classroom, we believe it is important to cue our students about our expectations from day one. Hispanic students, as well as other students, need to have high expectations articulated by the instructor both verbally and in written form. This approach not only includes reviewing the syllabus, class schedule, and grading criteria, but also includes explaining to students how they learn and how class time, exams, and assignments are structured to reflect the various levels of Bloom's taxonomy of learning domains (1956). Freshmen, for example, may be used to studying at the knowledge or comprehension levels of the taxonomy, and they need to know we expect them to perform at the application, analysis, synthesis, and evaluation levels. We expect this because we as instructors respect their ability to learn and to stretch themselves academically. Evaluations for both authors often state that our students were highly motivated both by our enthusiasm for the subject and by the challenge of really mastering the material. Although we have both heard that we "need to give these students a break" because of their disadvantaged background, we tell our students that giving them a break by expecting less from them is the worst kind of racism. Instead we tell them that they can learn difficult material and that they are just as capable of achieving academic excellence as students anywhere else.

Expecting students to maximize their potential is the underlying theme of our desire to help them learn how to reframe their learning experiences. Students need to know that just because material is difficult for them does not mean they are incapable of learning it or worse yet, that they are dumb. We tell them that the struggle *vale la pena* (is worth the effort) that they put into it because education should not be regurgitation. It is much more than that. The first author often tells the story of a sign on her professor's door that said, "Education Through Pain." Just as athletes work out their muscles and may have some pain as they improve their performance, the academic workout of the brain may also be a slow and painful process— that is, no pain, no gain. More important, as instructors we share our experiences as students and how we learned to learn. We talk about how we had to read and reread material in order to understand it, and about how education is not meant to be easy. If there is no challenge, there is no learning. This enables our students to know that struggling to learn is okay. Real learning takes effort, time, and commitment. They can choose how much and how well they are going to learn. As one student stated, "For some of us, a challenge seems more like a problem. But you [the instructor] help us look at it like more of a goal and a challenge. You help motivate us to look at this challenge more optimistically. Not every professor actually cares like you do!" Another student commented, "She pushes students to put forth [their] best work. [She] doesn't tolerate mediocre work."

Establishing credibility in the classroom is the last important component of creating a challenging classroom climate. So how do we as Hispanic women handle the issue of credibility? Sharing personal learning experiences with students helps us establish credibility on the basis of our knowledge, our expertise, and our relationships with them. In addition, we both deal with credibility building in the following ways: by being prepared, articulate, and knowledgeable; by treating students respectfully (goodwill); by providing honest feedback; and by being accessible and responsive to students. These are all behaviors that McCroskey (1998) discusses as important components of credibility for effective instructors.

What Are Effective "Consulting" Strategies for Creating a Positive Classroom Climate?

In this section we discuss our consulting strategies that empower our students and that encourage critical thinking and allow shared decision making in the classroom about the pace of the class, assignment due dates,

NEW DIRECTIONS FOR TEACHING AND LEARNING • DOI: 10.1002/tl

rewrite options, and so on. We provide a rationale for using these strategies as especially appropriate with Hispanic students, who usually come from families in which decisions are often made by the authority figure in the household. How this shared decision making helps to alleviate future problems is also discussed. In addition, we look at how to incorporate an honor system in the class, and why we use it for assignments and tests.

We define the term *consulting* in the most general sense, that is, we consult with our students by asking them their opinions and ideas about the teaching material and about classroom procedures such as due dates and so on. One effective consulting technique is the use of well-tailored questions that engage students in classroom interactions and help them develop critical thinking skills and the ability to respect different ideas. Thus questions are structured to elicit opinions and to encourage students to support their opinions using whatever evidence or supporting material that they have. Open-ended questions are most often used to start group discussion on particular concepts or issues. McCroskey (1998) has noted, "It is through disagreements that new ideas are generated and better ways to do things are learned" (p. 138). One student in an evaluation commented, "She encourages us to work with one another, allowing us to explore the possibilities of different views on various topics."

One way to set a classroom climate that encourages debate and constructive conflict is to structure the class as learning communities within the classroom and to articulate the expectations for behaviors up front (Book and Putman, 1992). These expectations include listening respectfully to others, focusing on the issues and not on personalities, agreeing to disagree agreeably, and respecting others' different perspectives. Having these guidelines has worked very well in our classrooms, as evidenced by the following student comment: "Putting us in groups allows [for our] empowerment." Another student wrote the following extensive comment:

> I know that normally I am not one to offer opinions, speak out in class, or even express my disagreement with views presented. This is because the typical classroom, elementary through college, . . . does not encourage independent thought, collaboration with classmates, or the fostering of meaningful relationships during class time. This instructor does all of this [sic]. In doing so, an extremely positive, friendly, and exciting environment is created, one where any contribution from each student is welcomed without the threat of ridicule, judgment, or criticism. The "round table" method is used just like in the time of King Arthur, where no one has more "power" than others. Everything that we do or is said is really a community effort. Having each of us choose group partners allows us freedom of choice and a sense of security.

As the preceding quote illustrates, the classroom climate is one of a partnership between the instructor and the students instead of a dictatorship. While the notion of using shared decision making in the classroom may seem strange, judicious use of this teaching strategy can prevent problems, encourage learning, and foster integrity in students. Most of our students work from twenty to forty or more hours a week. Most, we believe, want to do well in class. Family and work responsibilities, and time management issues, all contribute to their stress levels and their ability to learn the material; therefore our classes are structured so that students can, to a certain extent, have some flexibility on the exam and assignment due dates. Students are given choices about due dates, types of activities, and assignment topics early in the semester. Allowing their input and letting them have choices encourages students to take responsibility for their own learning.

To maintain the integrity of our teaching and our classroom community, we establish an honor code for take-home exams and for assignments. The honor statement is written by the students and signed prior to each assignment and examination to remind them that we trust them to do their own work. The results have been incredibly successful. Students actually wind up reading the book and learning the concepts instead of cramming and remembering the material just long enough for the class. The sense of accomplishment students feel when they have worked hard and done well helps motivate them even more. The use of the honor code helps them to develop good citizenship. They are proud of the fact that they have been trusted and that they have really learned the material instead of just memorizing it for the test. These consulting techniques for developing critical thinking skills and engendering responsibility and integrity can work with both small and large classes.

Conclusion

The purpose of this chapter has been to present some ideas about how two Hispanic women teaching at two institutions, each with a predominantly Hispanic population, create a classroom climate that effectively engages students while nurturing them and challenging them to succeed academically. We have also provided a review of literature that supports the instructor behaviors we use. Finally, we have included stories, student comments, and other examples to illustrate how creating a caring and challenging classroom can be accomplished via consultation with students. Overall our model of teaching is not the "sage on the stage" classical model that is so common in academe. Instead, we present ourselves as "facilitators of learning" who respect the wisdom our students bring with them. We prefer to serve as the "guides on the side" as we empower students to be responsible for their own learning and engaged in their own education.

References

Andersen, J. F. "Teacher Immediacy as a Predictor of Teaching Effectiveness." In D. Nimmo (ed.), *Communication Yearbook 3*. New Brunswick, N.J.: Transaction, 1979.
Bloom, B. S. *Taxonomy of Educational Objectives: Handbook 1: Cognitive Domain*. New York: David McKay, 1956.

Book, C. L., and Putman, J. G. "Organization and Management of a Classroom as a Learning Community Culture." In V. P. Richmond and J. C. McCroskey (eds.), *Power in the Classroom: Communication, Control, and Concern.* Hillsdale, N.J.: Erlbaum, 1992.

Javidi, M., Downs, V. C., and Nussbaum, J. F. "A Comparative Analysis of Teachers' Use of Dramatic Style Behaviors at Higher and Secondary Educational Levels." *Communication Education,* 1988, *37,* 278–288.

Kintsch, W., and Bates, E. "Recognition Memory for Statements from a Classroom Lecture." *Journal of Experimental Psychology: Human Learning and Memory,* 1977, *3,* 150–159.

Krathwohl, D. R., Bloom, B. S., and Masia, B. B. *Taxonomy of Educational Objectives. Handbook II: Affective Domain.* New York: David McKay, 1964.

McCroskey, J. C. *An Introduction to Communication in the Classroom.* (2nd ed.) Acton, Mass.: Tapestry Press, 1998.

Meier, R. S., and Feldhusen, J. F. "Another Look at Dr. Fox: Effect of Stated Purpose for Evaluation, Lecturer Expressiveness, and Density of Lecture Content on Student Ratings." *Journal of Educational Psychology,* 1979, *3,* 339–345.

Norton, R. *Communicator Style: Theory, Application, and Measures.* Beverly Hills, Calif.: Sage, 1983.

Norton, R., and Nussbaum, J. "Dramatic Behaviors of the Effective Teacher." In D. Nimmo (ed.), *Communication Yearbook 4.* New Brunswick, N.J.: Transaction, 1980.

Nussbaum, J. F. "Effective Teaching: A Communicative Nonrecursive Causal Model." In M. Burgoon (ed.), *Communication Yearbook 5.* New Brunswick, N.J.: Transaction, 1982.

Nussbaum, J. F. "Classroom Behaviors of the Effective Teacher." In D. Nimmo (ed.), *Communication Yearbook 4.* New Brunswick, N.J.: Transaction, 1984.

Nussbaum, J. F. "Effective Teacher Behaviors." *Communication Education,* 1992, *41,* 1992, 167–180.

Nussbaum, J. F., Comadena, M. E., and Holladay, S. J. "Classroom Verbal Behavior of Highly Effective Teachers." *Journal of Thought,* 1987, *22,* 73–80.

Perry, R. P., Abrami, P. C., and Levanthal, L. "Educational Seduction: The Effect of Instructor Expressiveness on Student Ratings and Achievement." *Journal of Educational Psychology,* 1979, *71,* 197–116.

Powers, W. G., Nitcavic, R., and Koerner, D. "Teacher Characteristics: A College Level Perspective." *Communication Education,* 1990, *39,* 227–233.

Sidelinger, R. J., and McCroskey, J. C. "Communication Correlates of Teacher Clarity in the College Classroom." *Communication Research Reports,* 1997, *14,* 1–10.

U.S. Bureau of the Census. *2000 Census of Population and Housing.* Washington, D.C.: U.S. Bureau of the Census, 2002. Retrieved Sept. 28, 2006, from http://www.census.gov/prod/cen2000.

DORA E. SAAVEDRA *is associate professor of communication at the University of Texas-Pan American.*

MARISA L. SAAVEDRA *is instructor of communication at South Texas College.*

9

In this chapter, the author explores student incivility in higher education, with an emphasis on the often hidden circumstance of students of color exhibiting disrespectful behavior toward their professors of the same race.

"She Must Be Trippin'": The Secret of Disrespect from Students of Color Toward Faculty of Color

Katherine Grace Hendrix

All teachers must be armed against engaging in student favoritism or in the practice of privileging some and ignoring the contributions of other students. The need to self-monitor to ensure fairness and keep one's biases under control is critical whether teaching kindergarten or a university-level graduate course. During my entire career as a female faculty member of color I have typically taught courses in which the majority of the students enrolled in the class were white and, as a result, have found myself addressing more complex issues associated with perceived favoritism toward particular students. More specifically, I have been keenly aware that my white students carefully observe my behavior to see if I will grant special favors to black students enrolled in the course. To maintain an atmosphere of fairness and to garner the trust of all of my students I occasionally announce in class that should a student come to me with special circumstances, I have one criterion: If another student made this request under the same situation, how would the issue be resolved? In short, what I would do for one student I would do for another, regardless of demographics.

For my nonblack students this was an indirect means of communicating my desire not to favor any single student or group of students enrolled in the class. For my black students it was a cue not to ask me for special favors such as, "Ahhh, Ms. Hendrix, give a brutha a break," or "Dr. Hendrix,

don't do me like that." Of course twenty-four years ago I took this stance to assist in establishing my credibility as a young black female instructor within the California community college system.

Students testing their limits and attempting to position themselves favorably is nothing new, and this behavior transcends race and gender. Male students attempt to flatter or intimidate female professors, female students flatter male professors and bond with female professors, and students of color establish a fictive kinship (see Fordham and Ogbu, 1986) based on perceived shared experiences of prejudice that may give them an "in" with professors of color.

The often unexplored question is, What happens when the perceived entitlement to favoritism transforms into disruptive, disrespectful student behavior? Research on disruptive behavior (also referred to as incivility, resistance, and reactive behavior) at the postsecondary level is gradually appearing in our scholarly journals (see Braxton and Bayer, 2004; Richardson, 1999). A special, often hidden form of incivility involves the problematic behavior of students of color toward their professors of the same race. In this chapter I provide a preliminary discussion of this issue by briefly (1) defining societal and classroom incivility (CI), (2) highlighting several examples of CI exhibited by black students toward black professors, (3) outlining three perspectives capable of informing an analysis of black student CI, and (4) suggesting how to address instances of black student CI. Although uncivil behaviors are generally inappropriate within the context of the professor-student relationship, they become even more problematic when the offender is of the same race.

Incivility Defined

Before addressing incivility in the classroom, we begin with a macroperspective, addressing the behavior of the U.S. citizenry. Sypher (2004, p. 257) states that we are engaged in a "battleground of colliding value systems and contentious discourse" in our workplaces that contributes to the coarsening of America (see Forni, 2002). Civility goes beyond politeness and manners to involve appropriately handling encounters with others, some degree of self-sacrifice (that is, restraint), and considering the needs of the collective.

Incivility, conversely, can be conceptualized as rude or disrespectful behavior without regard for the needs and feelings of others. Sypher (2004) provides examples of workplace incivility, including bullying, insensitivity, interrupting others, temper tantrums, emotional tirades, snippy e-mails, yelling, and questioning intentions and motives. *Desk rage* is defined as "emotional outbursts at work that negatively affect coworkers and the organization" (2004, p. 260). Incivility is rampant in our work environments, but because our vocations consume so much of our time, the workplace, ironically, is also where we attempt to meet our emotional needs. There is an increasingly blurred distinction between work and home, with workers increasingly feeling disconnected and disengaged, or as Palmer (2004) stated, living fractured, divided lives. Of course many of the individuals exposed to the stresses of road rage, family turmoil, and desk rage in turn enter our classrooms in the role of student exhibiting some of the same behaviors that have been carried out in their homes and cars and on the job.

Classroom Incivility (CI) Defined

According to Boice (1996), the intimidation and in some cases violence inflicted on high school teachers is often discussed, but unlike other professionals such as physicians and therapists, college professors rarely discuss incivility in higher education and, on those rare occasions when they do, they do so in an abstract manner. One potential reason for the absence or abstract discussion of postsecondary level CI is our desire as instructors to avoid appearing unable to control our students and thus to share a problem previously viewed as confined to the K–12 sector.

Chory-Assad and Paulsel (2004) used the term *antisocial classroom behavior* in their research investigating student responses to perceived classroom injustice. They found that student behaviors can be placed in one of three categories: (1) indirect interpersonal aggressiveness, (2) hostility, and (3) student resistance. Indirect interpersonal aggressiveness includes the active or passive act of harming another without engaging in face-to-face interaction (such as withholding information the instructor values, spreading rumors, or facilitating the instructor's failure). Hostility involves verbal, face-to-face behavior aimed directly at the professor. Student resistance disrupts on-task teaching and learning behavior and could include seeking revenge by lying about behavior, questioning the necessity of enacting particular behaviors, disrupting class, and getting even through complaints or negative teaching evaluations. The last category is distinguished from the other two on the basis of student behavior enacted with the primary intent of resisting an instructor's persuasive attempts to moderate the behavior.

The results of Boice's longitudinal study (1996) of sixteen professors over three years indicated that both teachers and students disliked loud, disruptive talk; loud groans; students making sarcastic remarks to professors; and "classroom terrorists" who exhibited unpredictable outbursts involving complaints and intimidating disagreements with the professor and fellow classmates. Students perceived CI in professors who were more than five minutes late to class, proffered surprise test items, belittled students, and were cold, distant teachers.[1] Related to the notion of professor CI, Kelsey, Kearney, Plax, and Allen (2001) found that teacher misbehaviors were interpreted as internal in origin, which they interpreted to be more salient than the positive teacher behaviors that convey immediacy (such as smiling, direct eye contact, and close proximity). In essence they found that "prior claims that implied that immediate teachers can escape assignments of negative attributions are not supported in this investigation. . . . Teacher immediacy cannot undo students' perceptions and attributions of negative teacher behavior" (p. 23). Thus acting appropriately and effectively in response to student CI and monitoring our own behavior in the classroom are of the utmost importance in maintaining our credibility and a classroom environment that is conducive to learning.

"She Must Be Trippin'": Black Students Manifesting CI

As I sat down one evening to work on this chapter, I pondered the notion of black students assuming that shared racial demographics and race-based prejudicial experiences automatically warranted them some special latitude. In essence, I reflected on being seen foremost not as their professor but rather as their "sistah girl," able to grant favors with reckless abandon, having no concern for the rest of my students. Interestingly, as I contemplated this notion of the "sistah girl," my phone rang and it was a longtime friend who is a college librarian. She called apologizing for not getting in touch sooner but explained that she was dealing with an extremely stressful situation—a group of black students who had been hastily enrolled in a special high school–community college degree program when the public protested the absence of black participants in the program. According to my friend, the students seemed to have been literally picked up off the street and put into the program without any assessment of their aptitude for the program's rigor.[2] To say the very least, it was ironic to have received a confirmation of what is addressed in this chapter.

Keeping in mind the construct of "sistah girl," let us explore three scenarios, including the one provided by my librarian friend.

Scene 1: A group of black students enter a community college library bringing paper plates, utensils, and food. They begin to disperse the dinnerware, and a black librarian approaches them indicating that food is not allowed in the library. They look at her as if to convey, "You've got to be kidding. *You* wouldn't do this to *us,* would you?" The stare down is followed by completely ignoring her request to exit the library or put away the food. The students continue to chat with one another and pass out their dinnerware in preparation for sharing lunch. After a second admonition is ignored, the black librarian calls security to have the students escorted from the premises. She is stressed, feels disrespected, and ironically also feels guilty for having to treat her own people in such a manner. Her coping mechanism: playing her jazz CDs until she wears them out.

Scene 2: This incident occurs at a historically black college with an instructor who is about twenty-five years of age and teaching with a master's degree. During an evening class the instructor critiques a black male student's speech and the student in turn becomes loud. He raises his voice in an angry tone while speaking to his instructor in front of the entire class. The young black instructor handles the situation by raising her voice as well, communicating that the student does not know her (an indication of the inappropriateness of his tone) and reminding the student that she is the authority figure in the class. Her coping mechanism: she excuses herself from the class and immediately seeks validation from her department chair regarding how the incident was handled.

Scene 3: A black female professor divides her class into small groups for an exercise. She has a particularly chatty black male student who loves interacting with the black female student who sits near him. As the class members move themselves into groups, the professor (anticipating what will ensue) asks the young man to join another group. The student gets up from his chair with much theatrical flair, changes his demeanor to convey his reluctance to move (by pushing a desk aside, dragging his feet, and swaggering as he moves toward the other group), and as he slowly joins another group loudly proclaims, "She *must* be *trippin'*," followed by a big smile and direct eye contact with his professor (signaling his triumph) once he hears several of his classmates giggle. Finding the student's behavior particularly amusing, the professor laughs and then says, "Well, that *may* be true, but do as I asked anyway!" Her coping mechanisms: being reminded of her extensive teaching experience, the comfort of tenure, and the confidence in her ability to be fair.

I am that female professor in scene 3, and the incident that occurred during the fall 2005 term serves as the motivation for this chapter. I have experienced numerous outbursts from students over my teaching career (as is the case for most professors) and have researched the phenomenon of black professors building credibility in predominantly white classrooms (Hendrix, 1997, 1998a, 1998b); however, I subconsciously tucked away in the recesses of my mind the phenomenon of black students' expectations of favoritism and their corresponding disrespect when those expectations are negated. Numerous sensibilities can be teased out when addressing this issue of black student CI: race-based similarities in how my students and I are perceived and treated by whites in U.S. society; a shared U.S. history as, most often, descendents of slaves; a desire for "my people" to excel and an obligation to move them forward; a pride in mentoring advanced black students; and a commitment to instilling confidence in those who perceive themselves as less capable. All of these notions related to racial solidarity must be considered in conjunction with my overall duties and responsibilities to the entire class, including (1) cultivating a safe place for discussion and learning, (2) providing an intellectually challenging course, (3) exhibiting interest and fairness, (4) teaching the curriculum (while slipping in racial tolerance), and (5) modeling inclusive, interpersonal instruction that entails teaching to a person, not just a "student." Articulating this assemblage of feelings and duties should give insight into the complexity of the problems of a black professor interacting with *some* black students enrolled in my courses.

NEW DIRECTIONS FOR TEACHING AND LEARNING • DOI: 10.1002/tl

The female professors in the first two scenarios are not only females in a traditionally male profession but also black females in a traditionally white male profession. As such, we must juggle a series of expectations from several groups requiring that we justify our existence to staff, administrators, and colleagues; convince our white students that we are qualified to teach at the collegiate level (this is especially true when the subject matter does not pertain directly to race); and in some cases persuade our black students that they must excel on the basis of merit rather than favoritism.

Possible Reasons for Student Perceptions

Due to the sparse research on collegiate level CI in general and on such behavior from students of color in particular, I draw from several bodies of research in order to offer potential explanations for black student CI, including adolescent development (Long, 1989), gender-related expectations (Sandler, 1991), Black identity development (Hardiman and Jackson, 1992; Jackson, 2001), and the Nigrescence Lifespan Model (Cross, 1991; Cross and Fhagen-Smith, 2001).

Long's work (1989) provides a macroperspective regarding student classroom behavior. According to Long, adolescents from puberty thru the late twenties are characterized by ambivalence (opposed feelings), and how such uncertainty is handled depends on their personality, intellect, sophistication, education, character, and rate of maturation. Thus, severe mood swings and unpredictable behavior can be expected from young people in this age group. Dziuban and Dziuban (1997–1998) outlined Long's four reactive behavior types: (1) aggressive-independents (AI), (2) aggressive-dependents (AD), (3) passive-independents (PI), and (4) passive-dependents (PD). Long stressed that each type has positive characteristics despite the presence in some cases of less impressive behaviors. AIs are impulsive and act and speak without considering the ramifications of their behavior; ADs are active participants who perform well and often set high goals for themselves; PIs have low needs for approval and minimal interest levels (disengaged in class); and PDs are gentle, sensitive, and unlikely to express any anger they may experience, and they aim to please.

Consistent with Long's findings, Dziuban (1996) found that 63 percent of the pupils identified as discipline problems were aggressive-independent, and Cioffi (1995) found that 81 percent of the high school students placed in gifted and advanced courses were aggressive-dependent. As noted by Dziuban and Dziuban (1997–1998), the personality types have important implications for higher education because each style manifests predictably different reactions to classroom material and teaching styles.

At about the same time as Long was investigating reactive behavior types and personality traits, Sandler (1991) chronicled the experiences of women in the classroom, indicating, as part of addressing the chilly classroom climate for women and minorities, that it was time to address "how students (male and female) treat women and men faculty differently" (p. 6). In her article, Sandler discussed the dissonance created by the presence of a woman in a traditionally male position, making a distinction between students' perceived appropriate societal female behavior (such as nurturing, hesitant, and intuitive) and those behaviors observed in the classroom (such as directness and rigor) that would be traditionally associated with males. As such, a female faculty member is an anomaly who does not act as expected and whose "very presence makes some of her students uncomfortable even before she speaks" (p. 11). Sandler attributes the differential (less respectful, more aggressive, attempts to intimidate, lower teaching evaluations) treatment of female faculty to society's devaluation of what women do in general, and to the comfort factor— being comfortable, as a woman, participating in courses taught by female faculty; comfortable, as a male, with challenging females; or uncomfortable in asserting oneself as a female faculty member.

Finally, several scholars have provided models and theories of identity development that are potentially applicable at the microlevel of the classroom to analyze young adult student behavior (Cross, 1991; Cross and Fhagen-Smith, 2001; Hardiman and Jackson, 1992; Jackson, 2001). Black identity development (BID) theory posits five stages of consciousness: (1) naiveté, (2) acceptance, (3) resistance, (4) redefinition, and (5) internalization. Of particular interest to this discussion are the resistance and redefinition stages. Jackson (2001, p. 22) states that "the Black person at *Resistance* recognizes to varying degrees and in a variety of situations, she or he can stop things from happening. For many, this is the first lesson in personal and social power.[3] Redefinition may follow the third stage, in which blacks define themselves independently of how they perceive whites and may be viewed as "separatists" or "self-segregating," whereas in the previous stage they may have been perceived as "troublemakers" (p. 24).

Jackson's counterparts have reconceptualized Cross's Nigrescence model (1991) to consider life stages rather than focusing on the adult experience of black identity development as did the original model. In their model of ego identity and Nigrescence, Cross and Fhagen-Smith (2001) acknowledge six sectors during the lifespan of blacks: (1) infancy and childhood, (2) preadolescence, (3) adolescence, (4) early adulthood, (5) adult Nigrescence, and (6) Nigrescence recycling. When explaining the third and fourth sectors, adolescence and early adulthood, the scholars say that "the great majority of Black youth [are] examining and struggling with issues of race and Black culture. . . . Upon leaving adolescence, young Black adults enter adult life with a spectrum of reference group orientations that tend to form three identity clusters" (Cross and Fhagen-Smith, 2001, p. 267): low salience identities, high race salience, and internalized racism (self-hatred). Hence students can enter our classrooms uninterested in race, resistant to what they perceive as white culture, or with low self-esteem.

NEW DIRECTIONS FOR TEACHING AND LEARNING • DOI: 10.1002/tl

Summary

These perspectives offer several viable explanations (meriting further investigation) for black students' disrespecting their black professors, ranging from the innocuous, understandable behavior experienced as they grow into adulthood, to a complex range of expected professor behavior that depends on how the student views his or her racial identity at his or her current stage of psychological, social, and racial development. Interestingly, Jackson notes that the emergence of ethnicity rather than race as a social organizer, Afrocentricity, and the U.S. economy (where class may bind us closer together than race) are contemporary influences possibly reshaping his theoretic model.

Discussion: Handling the Disruptive Student of Color

As women professors of color, our ability to address same-race student CI depends on numerous factors, including our age, years of teaching experience, departmental and campus reputation, tenure status, on- and off-campus support networks, and so on. For example, although I still think about the ramifications of what I might say to a student and of my end-of-the-term course evaluations, at this stage in my career I am in a "comfortable" position that affords me more leeway in what I can say and how. In addition, in the case of scene 3, I could laugh rather than cringe in disbelief as I would have in my early teaching days because (1) my teaching reputation and record of solid evaluations are established, (2) the student's behavior was no longer a novelty (been there, dealt with that), (3) I had learned not to take untoward student behavior as a personal affront in every instance, and (4) I was comfortable with my power and could more carefully decide when to demonstrate it. Nonetheless, in writing this chapter I have had to remember that every female professor of color is not in my current position, thereby necessitating a discussion of how to handle this particular type of classroom disruption.

Bad behavior is bad behavior regardless of race, and yet, as mentioned earlier, there are many nuances associated with *who* exhibits the behavior and with our initial response to the *what, how, where,* and *what next* questions that immediately flood our consciousness. Interestingly enough, for the black female professor two fundamental questions seem immediately to enter our consciousness regardless of the student's race: "Would she or he act this way if I were white? and Would she or he act this way with a male professor? The questions may be the same regardless of the perpetrator's race, but they emanate from markedly different planes of consciousness depending on *who* is misbehaving. In all cases we might wonder if the student feels that she or he can disrespect the authority of a black female, but in the case of bad behavior from black students we are also prone to speculate whether she or he is reacting to a failed attempt at negotiating bending (or breaking) the rules in the name of solidarity.

Holton's Model for Conflict Management (Holton, 1999) calls for a three-stage process for conflict resolution: (1) problem identification, (2) solution identification, and (3) solution implementation. Building on these basic principles, I would suggest foremost that professors of color recognize the importance of maintaining their professionalism. No matter how hostile and egregious the student of color's behavior, one must remain professional, which means that in-kind verbally aggressive (and certainly not physically aggressive) behavior is not allowed. With this cornerstone in place, I would suggest the following:

1. Do not shy away from assisting students of color and taking pride in their performance, but follow through on your responsibility to teach and encourage the entire class.
2. Consider discussing briefly at the onset of the term what you consider disrespectful behavior, and remind students of your expectations after witnessing several incidents of concern.
3. Do not overreact. Learn not to react to every perceived incident of CI, to avoid positioning yourself as an easy target. Recognize that some CI may be a bid for attention that can be easily resolved by involving the student in constructive, on-point class discussion.
4. Do not lose sight of the *individual;* recognize adolescent, psychological, and racial identity development as among the numerous contributing factors to your students behavior, and that race may or may not be applicable.
5. Address race-based requests immediately and in hearing distance of your class. Indicate that no one receives special favors, no matter how much you love or dislike a student, unless you are able to provide the same assistance to another student in the same circumstance.
6. Assert your authority using nonverbal cues (such as increased volume, movement toward the student, direct eye contact, or firm tone of voice).
7. When students are unresponsive to your nonverbal cues, accompany them with a brief statement responding to the student's request, question, or behavior, and immediately return to the lesson at hand.
8. E-mail and call students to come in for a private conference. This request can also be noted on an exam or homework assignment. Take the conference opportunity to ask the student to explain his or her behavior, and in turn share your perception and future expectations of the student. Decide if you want to speak to the most disruptive students individually or as a group. Determine if you want to speak to all of your black students or only those who are being disruptive.
9. Consider applying the Holton Model for Conflict Management in your classroom (see Holton, 1999).

NEW DIRECTIONS FOR TEACHING AND LEARNING • DOI: 10.1002/tl

10. Examine your verbal and nonverbal communication in the classroom and with your students of color. Ask yourself the following questions: In an effort to be seen as fair in the eyes of your white students, are you actually applying a more rigorous set of expectations to your students of color? Are you speaking to your students of color in a demeaning fashion? Are you trying to "relate" to the members of this classroom demographic? After some honest self-monitoring, adjust your behavior accordingly.
11. Step away from the situation and share the scenario with a trusted colleague, friend, or family member while asking for multiple ways to perceive the situation.
12. Document, document, document in case of a future grade complaint or retaliation on a teaching evaluation.
13. Learn from the successful and disastrous experiences, thereby preparing yourself to address successfully future instances of CI from your same-race students.

Conclusion

There are many satisfying moments as we engage our students in the postsecondary classroom, and the ability to care about, challenge, and consult with our students (see Chapter Eight in this volume) comes from expertise, preparation, and dedication to our profession. However, in the midst of our classroom triumphs there are also challenges—some totally unexpected that leave us mystified regarding the reasons for a student's behavior or academic performance. In my case, one of those mysteries has been uncivil behavior from students who are members of my own race. In this chapter I have shared the experiences of three women of color in order to initiate open dialogue and further investigation and analysis of the possible reasons (and resolutions) for such behavior. Keeping these incidents to myself, jotting them down in a journal, and occasionally whispering about them with another colleague of color did nothing to promote a better understanding of such untoward behavior, and little to improve on the phenomenon in higher education. Openness and honesty are now of paramount importance.

Notes

1. There are plenty of professors who are the root of incivility in their classroom or, at the very least, contribute to it. However, they are not the primary focus of this particular view of the problem.
2. Such behavior seems consistent with racist practices designed to put student-participants at a marked disadvantage (for example, the Tuskegee Airmen; see "Leadership Examples in Air Force Abundant Even if Unheralded," 2007). However, these students are of a different generation and as a result do not necessarily hold the same perspective as elderly family members regarding positively representing one's race.

3. Alexander (2004) perceived that black male student CI stemmed from resisting a white-focused curriculum or testing the alliance of black male professors.

References

Alexander, B. K. "Negotiating Cultural Identity in the Classroom." In M. Fong and R. Chuang (eds.), *Communicating Ethnic and Cultural Identity*. Lanham, Md.: Rowman & Littlefield, 2004.

Boice, B. "Classroom Incivilities." *Research in Higher Education*, 1996, 37, 453–486.

Braxton, J. M., and Bayer, A. E. (eds.). *Addressing Faculty and Student Classroom Improprieties*. New Directions for Teaching and Learning, no. 99. San Francisco: Jossey-Bass, 2004.

Chory-Assad, R. M., and Paulsel, M. L. "Classroom Justice: Student Aggression and Resistance as Reactions to Perceived Unfairness." *Communication Education*, 2004, 53, 253–273.

Cioffi, D. H. "A Description of Reactive Behavior Patterns in Gifted Adolescents." Unpublished doctoral dissertation, University of Central Florida, Orlando, 1995.

Cross, W. E., Jr. *Shades of Black: Diversity in African-American Identity*. Philadelphia: Temple University Press, 1991.

Cross, W. E., Jr., and Fhagen-Smith, P. "Patterns of African-American Identity Development: A Life Span Perspective." In C. L. Wijeyesinghe and B. W. Jackson, III (eds.), *New Perspectives on Racial Identity Development: A Theoretical and Practical Anthology*. New York: New York University Press, 2001.

Dziuban, J. I. "A Study of the Distribution of Reactive Behavior Patterns in Elementary Age Children and Their Relationship to Selected Demographics." Unpublished doctoral dissertation, University of Central Florida, Orlando, 1996.

Dziuban, J. I., and Dziuban, C. D. "Reactive Behavior Patterns in the Classroom." *Journal of Staff, Program, and Organization Development*, 1997–1998, 15, 85–91.

Fordham, S., and Ogbu, J. U. "Black Students' School Success: Coping with the Burden of 'Acting White.'" *Urban Review*, 1986, 18, 176–206.

Forni, P. M. *Choosing Civility*. New York: St. Martin's, 2002.

Hardiman, R., and Jackson, B. W., III. "Racial Identity Development: Understanding Racial Dynamics in College Classrooms and on Campus." In M. Adams (ed.), *Promoting Diversity in College Classrooms: Innovative Responses for the Curriculum, Faculty, and Institutions*. New Directions for Teaching and Learning, no. 52. San Francisco: Jossey-Bass, 1992.

Hendrix, K. G. "Student Perceptions of Verbal and Nonverbal Communication Cues Leading to Images of Professor Credibility." *Howard Journal of Communication*, 1997, 8, 251–274.

Hendrix, K. G. "Black and White Male Professor Perceptions of the Influence of Race on Classroom Dynamics and Credibility." *Negro Educational Review*, 1998a, 49, 37–52.

Hendrix, K. G. "Student Perceptions of the Influence of Race on Professor Credibility." *Journal of Black Studies*, 1998b, 28, 738–763.

Holton, S. A. "After the Eruption: Managing Conflict in the Classroom." In S. M. Richardson (ed.), *Promoting Civility: A Teaching Challenge*. New Directions for Teaching and Learning, no. 77. San Francisco: Jossey-Bass, 1999.

Jackson, B. W., III. "Black Identity Development: Further Analysis and Elaboration." In C. L. Wijeyesinghe and B. W. Jackson III (eds.), *New Perspectives on Racial Identity Development: A Theoretical and Practical Anthology*. New York: New York University Press, 2001.

Kelsey, D., Kearney, P., Plax, T. G., and Allen, T. H. "A Test-Retest of Teacher Misbehaviors." Paper presented at meeting of the National Communication Association, Atlanta, Ga., November 2001.

"Leadership Examples in Air Force Abundant Even if Unheralded." Retrieved May 5, 2007, from newsarchives.tamu.edu/stories/03/103003-7.html. Originally published on October 30, 2003, in *Aggie Daily Texas A&M University News*.

Long, W. A., Jr. "Personality and Learning: 1988 John Wilson Memorial Address." *Focus on Learning Problems in Math*, 1989, *11*, 1–16.

Palmer, P. J. *A Hidden Wholeness*. San Francisco: Jossey-Bass, 2004.

Richardson, S. M. (ed.). *Promoting Civility: A Teaching Challenge*. New Directions for Teaching and Learning, no. 77. San Francisco: Jossey-Bass, 1999.

Sandler, B. R. "Women Faculty at Work in the Classroom, or Why It Still Hurts to Be a Woman in Labor." *Communication Education*, 1991, *40*, 6–15.

Sypher, B. D. "Reclaiming Civil Discourse in the Workplace." *Southern Communication Journal*, 2004, *69*, 257–269.

KATHERINE GRACE HENDRIX is associate professor and former basic course director in the Department of Communication at the University of Memphis. She examines classroom credibility and the epistemological and axiological positions of research communities from a critical perspective.

NEW DIRECTIONS FOR TEACHING AND LEARNING • DOI: 10.1002/tl

Epilogue

Katherine Grace Hendrix

We came together in this issue to discuss the experiences of female faculty of color in postsecondary institutions and, in so doing, have articulated our experiences with student resistance, demonstrated our resilience, and identified our goals for the classroom experience and beyond. In this process of describing our individual experiences, we have created a collage of overlapping narratives that demonstrate our strength in the face of adversity and our resolve to create positive learning communities among our students and equip them not only with subject matter knowledge but also with an understanding and appreciation of inter- and cross-cultural relationships in the United States and abroad.

This collaboration has revealed a series of collective experiences that transcend age, nationality, ethnicity, race, years of teaching experience, and family status—experiences of student resistance to learning *from us* as African American, Arab, Brazilian, Chinese American, East Indian, Hispanic American, Japanese, and Taiwanese female faculty of color. However, comprehending that we may be our students' first encounter with a person of color in authority, we work to establish our credibility (and power) in order to enable the development of more open-minded students, promote effective teaching and learning, and establish our rightful position within academia.

We have offered our readers an accurate portrait of the postsecondary experience by presenting narratives that complement the existing, implicitly white male-focused teaching experience. Our hope is that the narratives in this volume have increased readers' knowledge of our contributions to education, in the United States and abroad, and imparted a clear repertoire of strategies for facilitating positive classroom environments and reducing student incivility. An additional goal is that, armed with this information, our readers, in their roles as colleagues and administrators, will strive to create an atmosphere of support and acknowledgment for us, an atmosphere that parallels our efforts as female faculty of color in higher education classrooms, departments, and campus meetings.

INDEX

Abraham, N., 26
Abrami, P. C., 78
Age and teaching, 9–10
Albert, R. D., 67, 68
Alexander, B. K., 95
Alexander-Snow, M., 69
Allen, T. H., 87
Andersen, J. F., 18, 77
Arab American professor's narrative, 25–32
Aries, E., 69
Asian female teachers: apprehension of, 5–12; autoethnography, 35–43; credibility of, 15–23
Australian education system, 46–47
Autoethnography of Chinese American professor, 35–43
Aznam, S., 48

Babcock, R., 50
Bandura, A., 67
Bartlett, L., 26, 27
Basow, S. A., 7, 8
Bates, E., 77
Bayer, A. E., 86
Beebe, S. A., 10
Bennett, S. K., 7
Bennington, L., 50
Bessant, J., 46, 47, 51
Bettencourt, B. A., 27, 29
Biernat, M., 27, 29
Billeaudeaux, A., 26
Billings, L. S., 27, 29
Black feminist thought and cultural contracts, 55–63
Black identity development (BID) theory, 91
Bloom, B. S., 78, 79, 82
Boice, B., 87
Boise, R., 69
Book, C. L., 81
Bradburn, E. M., 18
Braxton, J. M., 86
Brayboy, B. M., 26, 27
Bresnahan, M. I., 65, 67
Brislin, R. W., 68
Brown, S. V., 1
Burgoon, J. K., 27
Burkhalter, A. J., 69
Bush, G. W., 66

Campinha-Bacote, J., 70
Capotosto, L., 7
Carr, C., 58
Carter, K., 57
Centra, J. A., 7, 11
Chen, C., 1
Chory-Assad, R. M., 87
Cioffi, D. H., 90
Collier, M. J., 36
Collins, P. H., 56, 57, 60, 61, 63
Comadena, M. E., 77, 78
Competence: intercultural, 70; perceived, 68–69
Consulting strategies, 80–82
Crawley, R. L., 29, 30
Credibility: behaviors that establish, 80; defined, 17; dimensions of, 17–18; self-perceptions of, 19–20; students' perceptions of, 23
Critical race theory (CRT), 26–27
Cross, W. E., Jr., 90, 91
Cruz, C., 55
Cullen, D. L., 11
Cultural contracts theory, 57–58

Danowski, J., 28
De Simone, D. M., 7
Dean, A., 46
Dixson, A. D., 27
Domke, D., 26
Downs, V. C., 78
Du-Babcock, B., 50
Dziuban, C. D., 90
Dziuban, J. I., 90

Edwards, C., 9
Ethington, C. A., 7
Ethnicity and teaching, 8–9
Evans-Winters, V., 26, 30
Expectancy violation theory, 27–30

Fahimi, M., 18
Feagin, J. R., 55, 61
Feldhusen, J. F., 78
Feldmann, L. J., 37
Fhagen-Smith, P., 90, 91
Fister, D. L., 37
Fitch, F., 8
Fong, M., 35–43, 44
Fordham, S., 86

Forni, P. M., 86
Forrest Cataldi, E., 18
Foster, M., 1
Frymier, A. B., 18

Garland, P., 26
Garza, H., 35
Gasman, M., 55
Gaubatz, N. B., 7, 11
Gender and teaching, 7–8, 69
Globalization and American classrooms,
　66–68
Gonzalez, A., 1
Goodwin, L. D., 8, 10
Gorham, J., 18
Gudykunst, W. B., 67, 68

Hakim, C., 47
Hall, E. T., 18, 22
Hall, M. R., 18, 22
Hamilton, K., 7
Hanson, T. L., 16, 18
Hardiman, R., 90, 91
Hargett, J., 7
Harleston, B. W., 1
Harlow, R., 57, 60, 61
Harris, M. B., 2, 7
Harris, T. M., 55, 64
Harvey, W. B., 1
Harwood, J., 9
Hebbani, A. G., 2, 45, 53
Hendrix, K. G., 1, 2, 3, 7, 11, 23, 67, 85,
　89, 96, 97
Hernandez, T. J., 37
Hidalgo, N. M., 1
Hine, D. C., 55
Hispanic culture, teaching in a, 75–82
Hofstede, G., 2, 15, 16, 17, 23, 50
Holdridge, W., 17
Holladay, S. J., 77, 78
Holton, S. A., 93
Holton's Model for Conflict Manage-
　ment, 93
hooks, b., 56
Hopkins, S., 47
Houston, M., 1
Hsu, F., 50
Hutcheson, J., 26

Incivility, 85–94
Individualism-collectivism, 16
Intercultural competence, 70
Internationalization of college class-
　rooms, 65–73

Jackson, B. W., III, 90, 91, 92
Jackson, R. L., 1, 7, 29, 30, 57, 58, 59, 61
Javidi, M., 78
Johnson, S. D., 16, 18
Johnson-Bailey, J., 56, 61, 62

Karpin, D., 46
Kearney, P., 87
Kelsey, D., 87
Kenway, J., 71
Kiang, L., 58
Kibria, N., 58, 62
Kim, M. S., 65, 67
King, R., 39
Kintsch, W., 77
Kirtley, M. D., 8
Knowles, M. F., 1
Koerner, D., 78
Krathwohl, D. R., 78
Kuck, V. J., 7

Lackritz, J. R., 10, 11
Langan-Fox, J., 47
Le Roux, J., 55
Levanthal, L., 78
Lilley, R., 49
Lind, R., 28
Little, G., 28
Liu, S. X., 7
Long, W. A., Jr., 90
Luna, G., 11

MacLennan, J., 65
Marzabadi, C. H., 7
Masia, B. B., 78
Maslen, G., 51
McCalman, C. L., 2, 65, 74
McCroskey, J. S., 17, 67, 68, 76, 77, 80,
　81
McDowell, C. L., 1
McGray, D., 66
McLean, C. A., 15, 24
Medlock, A. L., 10
Meier, R. S., 78
Mestenhauser, J. A., 68
Meyer, J. P., 7
Meyers, C., 69
Miller, A. N., 16, 18
Modra, H., 71
Morgan, S. E., 8
Mottet, T. P., 10
Muhtaseb, A., 25, 33
Muslim Arab American professor's nar-
　rative, 25–32

Neuliep, J. W., 18, 67, 68
Niehoff, B. P., 23
Nitcavic, R., 78
Nolan, S. A., 7
Nonverbal immediacy, 18
Norton, R., 78
Nussbaum, J. F., 77, 78

Offshore teaching, 48–50
Ogbu, J. U., 86
Omi, M., 26
Otten, M., 66

Palmer, P. J., 87
Park, S. M., 10, 11
Patitu, C. L., 35
Paulsel, M. L., 87
Pearson, M., 48
Pennington, B., 68
Perry, R. P., 78
Phelan, J. E., 7
Plata, M., 35
Plax, T. G., 87
Poole, M. E., 47
Power distance, 17
Powers, W. G., 78
Professional title, use of, 57
Putman, J. G., 81

Raffeld, P. C., 10
Richardson, S. M., 86
Rousseau, C. K., 27
Rubenfeld, K., 8
Rubin, D. L., 66, 67

Saavedra, D. E., 2, 83
Saavedra, M. L., 2, 83
Sampson, S. N., 10
Sandler, B. R., 7, 90, 91
Schneider, A., 10
Schoen, L. G., 10
Sensenbaugh, R., 9
Shaheen, J. G., 28
Sheu, C., 23
Siddle, E. V., 1
Sidelinger, R. J., 77
Silberg, N. T., 7
Smart, J. C., 7
Smith, C., 9, 46
Smith, E., 57

Smith, J., 69
Smith, K. A., 66, 67
Spitzack, C., 57
Stangor, C., 58
Stevens, E. A., 8, 10
Student incivility, 85–94
Support groups, 72
Sypher, B. D., 86

Tack, M. W., 35
Tancred, P., 46
Tannen, D., 8
Teacher credibility: behaviors that estab-
    lish, 80; defined, 17; dimensions of,
    17–18; self-perceptions of, 19–20; stu-
    dents' perceptions of, 23
Teacher effectiveness, perceived, 67–68
Teacher immediacy, 18
Teacher self-efficacy, 10
Teaching behaviors, effective, 77–80
Teven, J. J., 16, 18
Thompson, C. A., 18
Title, use of professional, 57
Toomb, J. K., 17
Turnley, W. H., 23

Uncertainty avoidance, 16–17

Valencia, R. R., 27
Vandenbroeck, M., 62
Vasil, L., 10
Vescio, T. K., 27, 29

Warren, J. R., 1, 7
Weaver, J. B., 8
Wei, F-Y. F., 5, 14
White, K., 46, 47, 51
Wildermuth, S., 68
Williams, D. G., 26, 30
Winant, H., 26
Winocur, S., 10
Witt, S., 57
Wood, J., 70

Xu, L., 50

Yen, H.J.R., 23
Yook, E. L., 67, 68

Zeltman, M. L., 7

OTHER TITLES AVAILABLE IN THE
NEW DIRECTIONS FOR TEACHING AND LEARNING SERIES
Marilla D. Svinicki, Editor-in-Chief
R. Eugene Rice, Consulting Editor

TL108   Developing Student Expertise and Community: Lessons from How People
         Learn
         Anthony J. Petrosino, Taylor Martin, Vanessa Svihla
         This issue presents research from a collaboration among learning scientists,
         assessment experts, technologists, and subject-matter experts, with the goal
         of producing adaptive expertise in students. The model is based on the
         National Research Council book *How People Learn*. The chapters present
         case studies of working together to develop learning environments centered
         on challenge-based instruction. While the strategies and research come from
         engineering, they are applicable across disciplines to help students think
         about the process of problem solving.
         ISBN: 07879-9574-6

TL107   Exploring Research-Based Teaching
         Carolin Kreber
         Investigates the wide scope research-based teaching, while focusing on two
         distinct forms. The first sees research-based teaching as student-focused,
         inquiry-based learning; students become generators of knowledge. The
         second perspective fixes the lens on teachers; the teaching is characterized
         by discipline-specific inquiry into the teaching process itself. Both methods
         have positive effects on student learning, and this volume explores research
         and case studies.
         ISBN: 07879-9077-9

TL106   Supplemental Instruction: New Visions for Empowering Student Learning
         Marion E. Stone, Glen Jacobs
         Supplemental Instruction (SI) is an academic support model introduced over
         thirty years ago to help students be successful in difficult courses. SI teaches
         students how to learn via regularly scheduled, out-of-class collaborative
         sessions with other students. This volume both introduces the tenets of SI to
         beginners and brings those familiar up to speed with today's methods and
         the future directions. Includes case studies, how-to's, benefits to students
         and faculty, and more.
         ISBN: 0-7879-8680-1

TL105   A Laboratory for Public Scholarship and Democracy
         Rosa A. Eberly, Jeremy Cohen
         Public scholarship has grown out of the scholarship-and-service model, but
         its end is democracy rather than volunteerism. The academy has intellectual
         and creative resources that can help build involved, democratic communities
         through public scholarship. Chapters present concepts, processes, and case
         studies from Penn State's experience with public scholarship.
         ISBN: 0-7879-8530-9

TL104   Spirituality in Higher Education
         Sherry L. Hoppe, Bruce W. Speck
         With chapters by faculty and administrators, this book investigates the role
         of spirituality in educating the whole student while recognizing that how

spirituality is viewed, taught, and experienced is intensely personal. The goal is not to prescribe a method for integrating spirituality but to offer options and perspectives. Readers will be reminded that the quest for truth and meaning, not the destination, is what is vitally important.
ISBN: 0-7879-8363-2

TL103   **Identity, Learning, and the Liberal Arts**
Ned Scott Laff
Argues that we must foster conversations between liberal studies and student development theory, because the skills inherent in liberal learning are the same skills used for personal development. Students need to experience core learning that truly influences their critical thinking skills, character development, and ethics. Educators need to design student learning encounters that develop these areas. This volume gives examples of how liberal arts education can be a healthy foundation for life skills.
ISBN: 0-7879-8333-0

TL102   **Advancing Faculty Learning Through Interdisciplinary Collaboration**
Elizabeth G. Creamer, Lisa R. Lattuca
Explores why stakeholders in higher education should refocus attention on collaboration as a form of faculty learning. Chapters give theoretical basis then practical case studies for collaboration's benefits in outreach, scholarship, and teaching. Also discusses impacts on education policy, faculty hiring and development, and assessment of collaborative work.
ISBN: 0-7879-8070-6

TL101   **Enhancing Learning with Laptops in the Classroom**
Linda B. Nilson, Barbara E. Weaver
This volume contains case studies—mostly from Clemson University's leading-edge laptop program—that address victories as well as glitches in teaching with laptop computers in the classroom. Disciplines using laptops include psychology, music, statistics, animal sciences, and humanities. The volume also advises faculty on making a laptop mandate successful at their university, with practical guidance for both pedagogy and student learning.
ISBN: 0-7879-8049-8

TL100   **Alternative Strategies for Evaluating Student Learning**
Michelle V. Achacoso, Marilla D. Svinicki
Teaching methods are adapting to the modern era, but innovation in assessment of student learning lags behind. This volume examines theory and practical examples of creative new methods of evaluation, including authentic testing, testing with multimedia, portfolios, group exams, visual synthesis, and performance-based testing. Also investigates improving students' ability to take and learn from tests, before and after.
ISBN: 0-7879-7970-8

TL99   **Addressing Faculty and Student Classroom Improprieties**
John M. Braxton, Alan E. Bayer
Covers the results of a large research study on occurrence and perceptions of classroom improprieties by both students and faculty. When classroom norms are violated, all parties in a classroom are affected, and teaching and learning suffer. The authors offer guidelines for both student and faculty classroom behavior and how institutions might implement those suggestions.
ISBN: 0-7879-7794-2

TL98 **Decoding the Disciplines: Helping Students Learn Disciplinary Ways of Thinking**
David Pace, Joan Middendorf
The Decoding the Disciplines model is a way to teach students the critical-thinking skills required to understand their specific discipline. Faculty define bottlenecks to learning, dissect the ways experts deal with the problematic issues, and invent ways to model experts' thinking for students. Chapters are written by faculty in diverse fields who successfully used these methods and became involved in the scholarship of teaching and learning.
ISBN: 0-7879-7789-6

TL97 **Building Faculty Learning Communities**
Milton D. Cox, Laurie Richlin
A very effective way to address institutional challenges is a faculty learning community. FLCs are useful for preparing future faculty, reinvigorating senior faculty, and implementing new courses, curricula, or campus initiatives. The results of FLCs parallel those of student learning communities, such as retention, deeper learning, respect for others, and greater civic participation. This volume describes FLCs from a practitioner's perspective, with plenty of advice, wisdom, and lessons for starting your own FLC.
ISBN: 0-7879-7568-0

TL96 **Online Student Ratings of Instruction**
Trav D. Johnson, D. Lynn Sorenson
Many institutions are adopting Web-based student ratings of instruction, or are considering doing it, because online systems have the potential to save time and money among other benefits. But they also present a number of challenges. The authors of this volume have firsthand experience with electronic ratings of instruction. They identify the advantages, consider costs and benefits, explain their solutions, and provide recommendations on how to facilitate online ratings.
ISBN: 0-7879-7262-2

TL95 **Problem-Based Learning in the Information Age**
Dave S. Knowlton, David C. Sharp
Provides information about theories and practices associated with problem-based learning, a pedagogy that allows students to become more engaged in their own education by actively interpreting information. Today's professors are adopting problem-based learning across all disciplines to faciliate a broader, modern definition of what it means to learn. Authors provide practical experience about designing useful problems, creating conducive learning environments, facilitating students' activities, and assessing students' efforts at problem solving.
ISBN: 0-7879-7172-3

TL94 **Technology: Taking the Distance out of Learning**
Margit Misangyi Watts
This volume addresses the possibilities and challenges of computer technology in higher education. The contributors examine the pressures to use technology, the reasons not to, the benefits of it, the feeling of being a learner as well as a teacher, the role of distance education, and the place of computers in the modern world. Rather than discussing only specific successes or failures, this issue addresses computers as a new cultural

symbol and begins meaningful conversations about technology in general and how it affects education in particular.
ISBN: 0-7879-6989-3

TL93   **Valuing and Supporting Undergraduate Research**
Joyce Kinkead
The authors gathered in this volume share a deep belief in the value of undergraduate research. Research helps students develop skills in problem solving, critical thinking, and communication, and undergraduate researchers' work can contribute to an institution's quest to further knowledge and help meet societal challenges. Chapters provide an overview of undergraduate research, explore programs at different types of institutions, and offer suggestions on how faculty members can find ways to work with undergraduate researchers.
ISBN: 0-7879-6907-9

TL92   **The Importance of Physical Space in Creating Supportive Learning Environments**
Nancy Van Note Chism, Deborah J. Bickford
The lack of extensive dialogue on the importance of learning spaces in higher education environments prompted the essays in this volume. Chapter authors look at the topic of learning spaces from a variety of perspectives, elaborating on the relationship between physical space and learning, arguing for an expanded notion of the concept of learning spaces and furnishings, talking about the context within which decision making for learning spaces takes place, and discussing promising approaches to the renovation of old learning spaces and the construction of new ones.
ISBN: 0-7879-6344-5

TL91   **Assessment Strategies for the On-Line Class: From Theory to Practice**
Rebecca S. Anderson, John F. Bauer, Bruce W. Speck
Addresses the kinds of questions that instructors need to ask themselves as they begin to move at least part of their students' work to an on-line format. Presents an initial overview of the need for evaluating students' on-line work with the same care that instructors give to the work in hard-copy format. Helps guide instructors who are considering using on-line learning in conjunction with their regular classes, as well as those interested in going totally on-line.
ISBN: 0-7879-6343-7

TL90   **Scholarship in the Postmodern Era: New Venues, New Values, New Visions**
Kenneth J. Zahorski
A little over a decade ago, Ernest Boyer's *Scholarship Reconsidered* burst upon the academic scene, igniting a robust national conversation that maintains its vitality to this day. This volume aims at advancing that important conversation. Its first section focuses on the new settings and circumstances in which the act of scholarship is being played out; its second identifies and explores the fresh set of values currently informing today's scholarly practices; and its third looks to the future of scholarship, identifying trends, causative factors, and potentialities that promise to shape scholars and their scholarship in the new millennium.
ISBN: 0-7879-6293-7

TL89 Applying the Science of Learning to University Teaching and Beyond
Diane F. Halpern, Milton D. Hakel
Seeks to build on empirically validated learning activities to enhance what and how much is learned and how well and how long it is remembered. Demonstrates that the movement for a real science of learning—the application of scientific principles to the study of learning—has taken hold both under the controlled conditions of the laboratory and in the messy real-world settings where most of us go about the business of teaching and learning.
ISBN: 0-7879-5791-7

TL88 Fresh Approaches to the Evaluation of Teaching
Christopher Knapper, Patricia Cranton
Describes a number of alternative approaches, including interpretive and critical evaluation, use of teaching portfolios and teaching awards, performance indicators and learning outcomes, technology-mediated evaluation systems, and the role of teacher accreditation and teaching scholarship in instructional evaluation.
ISBN: 0-7879-5789-5

TL87 Techniques and Strategies for Interpreting Student Evaluations
Karron G. Lewis
Focuses on all phases of the student rating process—from data-gathering methods to presentation of results. Topics include methods of encouraging meaningful evaluations, mid-semester feedback, uses of quality teams and focus groups, and creating questions that target individual faculty needs and interest.
ISBN: 0-7879-5789-5

TL86 Scholarship Revisited: Perspectives on the Scholarship of Teaching
Carolin Kreber
Presents the outcomes of a Delphi Study conducted by an international panel of academics working in faculty evaluation scholarship and postsecondary teaching and learning. Identifies the important components of scholarship of teaching, defines its characteristics and outcomes, and explores its most pressing issues.
ISBN: 0-7879-5447-0

TL85 Beyond Teaching to Mentoring
Alice G. Reinarz, Eric R. White
Offers guidelines to optimizing student learning through classroom activities as well as peer, faculty, and professional mentoring. Addresses mentoring techniques in technical training, undergraduate business, science, and liberal arts studies, health professions, international study, and interdisciplinary work.
ISBN: 0-7879-5617-1

TL84 Principles of Effective Teaching in the Online Classroom
Renée E. Weiss, Dave S. Knowlton, Bruce W. Speck
Discusses structuring the online course, utilizing resources from the World Wide Web and using other electronic tools and technology to enhance classroom efficiency. Addresses challenges unique to the online classroom community, including successful communication strategies, performance evaluation, academic integrity, and accessibility for disabled students.
ISBN: 0-7879-5615-5

TL83   Evaluating Teaching in Higher Education: A Vision for the Future
        Katherine E. Ryan
        Analyzes the strengths and weaknesses of current approaches to evaluating
        teaching and recommends practical strategies for improving current
        evaluation methods and developing new ones. Provides an overview of new
        techniques such as peer evaluations, portfolios, and student ratings of
        instructors and technologies.
        ISBN: 0-7879-5448-9

TL82   Teaching to Promote Intellectual and Personal Maturity: Incorporating
        Students' Worldviews and Identities into the Learning Process
        Marcia B. Baxter Magolda
        Explores cognitive and emotional dimensions that influence how individuals
        learn, and describes teaching practices for building on these to help students
        develop intellectually and personally. Examines how students' unique
        understanding of their individual experience, themselves, and the ways
        knowledge is constructed can mediate learning.
        ISBN: 0-7879-5446-2

NEW DIRECTIONS FOR TEACHING AND LEARNING
Order Form
SUBSCRIPTIONS AND SINGLE ISSUES

DISCOUNTED BACK ISSUES:

Use this form to receive **20% off** all back issues of New Directions for Teaching and Learning. All single issues priced at **$23.20** (normally $29.00)

TITLE	ISSUE NO.	ISBN
_____	_____	_____
_____	_____	_____
_____	_____	_____

Call 888-378-2537 or see mailing instructions below. When calling, mention the promotional code, JB7ND, to receive your discount.

SUBSCRIPTIONS: *(1 year, 4 issues)*

☐ New Order   ☐ Renewal

U.S.	☐ Individual: $80	☐ Institutional: $195
Canada/Mexico	☐ Individual: $80	☐ Institutional: $235
All Others	☐ Individual: $104	☐ Institutional: $269

Call 888-378-2537 or see mailing and pricing instructions below. Online subscriptions are available at www.interscience.wiley.com.

Copy or detach page and send to:
John Wiley & Sons, Journals Dept, 5th Floor
989 Market Street, San Francisco, CA 94103-1741

Order Form can also be faxed to: 888-481-2665

Issue/Subscription Amount: $ _____	**SHIPPING CHARGES:**	
Shipping Amount: $ _____	SURFACE	Domestic Canadian
(for single issues only—subscription prices include shipping)	First Item	$5.00 $6.00
Total Amount: $ _____	Each Add'l Item	$3.00 $1.50

(No sales tax for U.S. subscriptions. Canadian residents, add GST for subscription orders. Individual rate subscriptions must be paid by personal check or credit card. Individual rate subscriptions may not be resold as library copies.)

☐ Payment enclosed (U.S. check or money order only. All payments must be in U.S. dollars.)

☐ VISA   ☐ MC   ☐ Amex # _____ Exp. Date _____

Card Holder Name _____ Card Issue # _____

Signature _____ Day Phone _____

☐ Bill Me (U.S. institutional orders only. Purchase order required.)

Purchase order # _____
Federal Tax ID13559302   GST 89102 8052

Name _____

Address _____

Phone _____ E-mail _____

JB7ND

Made in the USA
Lexington, KY
18 February 2017